CASTLE HOUSE
BUCKINGHAM

Castle House, 2006

CASTLE HOUSE
BUCKINGHAM
A comfortable family residence

JULIAN HUNT AND JOHN CLARKE

To Prue
Best Wishes
from
Bendan 2007

Phillimore

2007

Published by
PHILLIMORE & CO. LTD
Shopwyke Manor Barn, Chichester, West Sussex, England
www.phillimore.co.uk

ISBN 978-1-86077-449-2

Printed and bound in Great Britain

CONTENTS

LIST OF ILLUSTRATIONS

ACKNOWLEDGEMENTS

The authors would like to thank Mrs Barbara Edmondson for setting the challenge of chronicling such an exciting and unusual building as Castle House. They would also like to thank personally her son David Edmondson and the staff at Castle House, especially Liz Wickham, Cynthia Robinson and Glynis Simpkin, for their unstinting hospitality during the research and production of this book.

Thanks are due to Roger Bettridge and the staff of the Centre for Buckinghamshire Studies for their continued support and for permission to reproduce photographs of Castle House in 1912 and 1948; to Aylesbury Vale District Council for access to their deeds to Castle House; to the National Monuments Record at Swindon for permission to reproduce photographs taken during the survey of Castle House in 1912; to Alan Petford for re-surveying the west wing of Castle House, his advice on architectural and historical matters, and for permission to use his slides taken in 2005; to James Hearn and Simon Hearn for information on, and photographs of, the Hearn family; to Valerie Woodings, Rosemary Carter, Michael and Anne Pinkerton for recollections and photographs of the Bull family; to Nancy Lady Bagot for photographs of paintings of Sir Edward and Lady Mary Bagot; to John Credland for the photograph used on the dust jacket; to Brian Mingham of Lorimers solicitors for information on the Hearn family; to Paul Woodfield for information on the architect Edward Swinfen Harris; to Mavis Briars for information on the Barton family; to Peter and Honor Lowless for advice on Adams v. Lambert; Mike Malone for making contacts with the Hearn family, Paul Poornan for sharing his knowledge of the history of Buckingham, Lyn Robinson for finding the grave of Thomas Bucks, and Toni Clemence for tending the gardens of Castle House.

FOREWORD

I WAS BORN on 1 September 1925 at Collingbourne Ducis, a village on the edge of Pewsey Vale, in Wiltshire. My father rented a small farm called Mount Orleans. In 1931, however, my parents moved to St Albans, in Hertfordshire, where my father took on a dairy business. I was educated at St Albans High School for Girls where I enjoyed my school days. My interest in biology, which included human anatomy, certainly influenced my decision to go in for a nursing career. I also wished to gain qualifications to rely on in the future.

In 1944 I commenced my training at St George's Hospital, Hyde Park Corner. By 1950 I had qualified as a State Registered Nurse and as a State Registered Midwife. One day, a patient who worked for the Anglo-Iranian Oil Company suggested that I should consider becoming a Nursing Sister at the Hospital attached to the oil refinery in Abadan, in South Persia. I decided that this was a good idea and on 15 June 1950 – in the heat of the summer – I arrived in Persia by air. There was a wonderful social life and I soon met Derek Edmondson, a junior executive with the Anglo-Iranian Oil Company. He was two years younger than me, but we married on 8 September 1951 at St Michael's Church, St Albans.

Derek then joined the Crittall Manufacturing Company and in 1953, at the time of the Mau Mau emergency, he was posted to Nairobi, Kenya. In Kenya, I worked with Dr Michael Wood, the founder of the East Africa Flying Doctor Service; Dr Wood flew himself in his own plane. In 1954 Derek became Managing Director of Crittall Malaysia Ltd in Singapore. There, I worked as a Nursing Sister at the private Nursing Home of Dr Stanley Pavillard. We were still in Singapore in 1959, when the colony gained independence. Along with several other British people, we joined the exodus over the Causeway into Johore, and thus to Malaya. Our son Richard was born in Singapore in 1956. Our second son David was born at home in St Albans in 1957, but our daughter Hilary was born in Kuala Lumpur in 1965. Derek set up factories in Petaling Jaya, Malaysia and near Bangkok, Thailand. In recognition of his contribution to British Industry, Derek was awarded an MBE by the Queen. He received the award at Government House in central Sydney, which was splendid as we were about to move on to Australia.

In 1969 Derek and I bought a derelict house in the north shore suburb of Pymble, Sydney. The restoration took five years, but it gave me the opportunity to develop my skills in finding materials and organising building work. Derek was now travelling across the world for weeks at a time as financial director of Pillar Naco Holdings, a subsidiary of Rio Tinto Zinc. In 1973, however, we had to leave Australia when Derek changed his job. He joined the Charterhouse Banking Group and became Managing Director of Charterhouse Middle East Ltd. Once again,

1   Derek Edmondson, Abadan, 1950

there was a chance to live abroad, and we were dispatched to South Africa. We found an English-style thatched cottage, owned by the mother-in-law of Vie Guhr, the wildlife artist, on the outskirts of Johannesburg. After several months in South Africa, following the sale of a large hotel chain, we moved to Teheran to set up a new office. Next we were transferred to the United Arab Emirates to set up companies with Arab partners. We were based in Sharjah, once one of the Trucial States. There were problems with the bare skeleton of a new duplex house. Cupboards and equipment for an office were necessary and in came the practical side of Derek Edmondson. We put in a small swimming pool, inserted into an area of pure sand. It was very enjoyable to search for plants and shrubs for a green surrounding area and I learnt more about finding discarded vegetation and suitable cardboard as biodegradable materials for composting. We became increasingly resourceful and, then and later, this allowed us to achieve much more than we could have otherwise afforded.

In February 1978, we returned to England, where we would finally make a permanent home. We were determined not to waste the skills we had amassed in restoring houses in other countries but, at first, we could not find a suitable house needing restoration within reach of London. In June 1978, however, a telephone call to Aylesbury led us to an agent who had just received brochures from Aylesbury Vale District Council announcing the sale of Castle House, Buckingham, a Grade II* listed building. After many visits, the fourth with an architect, we decided to make an offer. This was accepted provisionally, but before everything could be settled, we had to satisfy the Council that we would keep to some quite specific building regulations. Finally, the District Council conveyed the property to us on 8 December 1978.

During our earlier visits, we had not been allowed to see the delightful central room with French windows looking into the garden. This was then the Mayor's Parlour. But, eventually, we met the Mayor, the charming Miss Mary McManus, and she took us in. There were many people in Buckingham who feared that the town was about to lose its most historic house and, when I told Miss McManus that we had definitely decided to buy the house, she exclaimed, 'It's a miracle, it's a miracle.' These are words I can never forget and they described our feelings too. We also received a warm welcome from the Deputy Mayor, Mrs Mary O'Hara, wife of the Reverend Michael O'Hara, Minister of the United Reform Church. We were invited to an Edwardian garden party in aid of the church and met several people who were to become our friends, including Mrs Daphne Lorimer, Mrs Ruby Lines, Mrs

Gwendoline Hounslow and Mrs Mary Buckingham.

We moved in during the cold of winter, with no furniture. To begin with, we slept on mattresses on the floors of various rooms. We soon realised that the old and massive central heating system could never function again. It was so cold and draughty that we began to wonder whether the stories we had heard from the Paranormal Society about the ghost of the chaplain of Catherine of Aragon might be true after all. The derelict outhouses, the crumbling ivy-clad walls and owls at night gave Castle House something of the feeling of a set from a horror movie. But we had to turn it into a happy family home – as it had once been for many, though sadly not for all, of its previous owners.

We began to restore Castle House in 1979. We needed to find assistance to help

2   Barbara Edmondson, c.1951

us with the many heavy tasks to be undertaken. We knew that this initial period of the restoration would be crucial. If we took the wrong decisions the whole project could easily have turned into a disaster. We began to record our ideas, making sketches to scale and collecting samples of existing materials such as wall-paper and paintwork. There were old fan-lights and fittings, such as hinges and locks, to be removed but stored carefully for use later. There were many difficult decisions to be made: should we try to preserve lath-and-plaster ceilings or install new ceiling board; where should light fittings and power points be located; should we keep tile or wooden floors or carpet them over? We needed to decide what materials were to be used for fireplace surrounds, chimney pieces and hearths – marble or Hornton stone? There were so many decisions but I think we got most of them right.

Heating proved an especially difficult problem: what form; where radiators should be placed; arrangements for temperature controls, etc. While we wanted to retain as much as possible from the old house, it was inevitable that a great deal of material would have to be removed to make way for more modern facilities. I was amazed at the amount of lead piping and water tanks that we encountered in the closets and elsewhere. So much lead could have been a health hazard – but it required huge efforts to remove the lead and the heavy, iron, wide-bore central heating pipes. Two strong men, armed with special double wrenches, found it hard going to undo the joints. And as for the central heating boiler itself ... One large skip proved insufficient to take the lead alone. The dust and rubbish below the floor-boards, especially in the attic, took weeks to remove. The work could only be done manually with heads covered and scarves or masks round mouth and nostrils. There were many surprises. Under the totally rotten floor of the Mayor's Parlour we found disintegrated chicken bones among the dirt – perhaps discarded after feasts held centuries earlier? One rather more pleasant surprise was a huge open fireplace, complete with a massive beam supporting the chimney, and a cavity for a bread oven.

My husband engaged John Meadows, with his young apprentice, Tim Williams, to do much of the work, and later on Richard Marston. But there were many other helpers. My son Richard and his family worked on the east wing, and my daughter Hilary regarded the attic in the west wing as her own. There were various experienced craftsmen, such as plumbers, electricians, plasterers, brick-layers, painters, stone-masons and glass cutters and fitters, who came and went. I don't think I could count them all but there must have been a huge number of splendid and conscientious people who have worked on the house from 1979 until the present.

We thought it would take five years to restore Castle House but we came to realise that we would never finish the job. My husband died in November 1993, but I pressed on with the task of preserving the house and researching its past. Over the years, many descendants of the families who lived at Castle House have visited me and helped me to piece its history together. There is always something more to find out, but the time has come to draw a line and get the story into print. I hope this book on Castle House will help others in Buckingham and beyond to share the pleasure we have had as custodians of this great house.

Barbara Edmondson, 2006

What's in a Name?

CASTLE HOUSE was anciently the home of the Bartons, the Fowlers and the Lamberts, three of the most notable families in the history of Buckingham. In the oldest parts of the house, dating from the 15th century, datestones with the initials 'W.L.M.', feature prominently and refer to the rebuilding by William and Mary Lambert in the time of James I. At least since the 17th century, Castle House has had no rival in the town. It is unquestionably the finest house in 'The Loyal and Ancient Borough of Buckingham'.

Although Castle House is of undoubted antiquity, we look in vain for any clear reference to it by that name before the 19th century. That is not to say that Castle House lacks early documentation; on the contrary, there is an abundance of information. Yet, in earlier times, what we now know as Castle House was usually referred to as the 'capital mansion' of the Bartons, Fowlers or Lamberts, or as 'Fowlers Farm in West Street, alias Fowlers Street'. The fact that one of these family names was also attached to the street provides strong evidence of the importance of the house and of the high status of its various owners. Does it matter then that the name 'Castle House' is a relatively modern one?

'A Rose by any other Name'

In *Romeo and Juliet*, Shakespeare asks 'What's in a name?' To begin with he implies that names do not matter – 'A rose by any other name would smell as sweet'. But then he goes on to say that names do matter. There is something in a name that reflects the very being or essence of the thing it describes. But what of Castle House? Anyone hearing the name Castle House will be looking for battlements rather than sash windows.

Let us consider the two words 'Castle' and 'House'. If not exactly oxymoronic, there is a definite tension between the two words. 'Castle' implies something large, a building with turrets and draw-bridges, whose ultimate function is military. Considerations of comfort must yield to those of security. Castles are cold, often damp and usually draughty. But 'House' implies safety and comfort; in our mind's eye we see a domestic place, a place for husbands and wives, for growing families, a place for the entertainment of guests. There have been times when Castle House *was* quite grand, but it has never been anyone's idea of a Castle. First and foremost it has always been a house. But why call it 'Castle House'?

In the Middle Ages there was certainly a castle in Buckingham. Even today, there is a Castle Street and, until recently, the *Villiers Hotel* was known as the 'Swan and Castle'. But Castle House is not on the same site as Buckingham Castle. Its location is entirely without military advantages. At Castle House the land is at the bottom of a hill and there is no protection offered by the river. It would have made no sense at all to build a castle there. Buckingham Castle was on a piece of higher ground – where the present Church of St Peter and St Paul stands – a natural promontory surrounded on three sides by the River Ouse. It was actually a rather good site for a castle. If you look over the railings on the east side of the church, you can see how steep the bank is down to Well Street. It would have been extremely difficult for an attacking force to storm its way up.

Browne Willis

The first mention of the term 'Castle House' is in Browne Willis's *History and Antiquities of the Town, Hundred and Deanery of Buckingham*, published in 1755. On page 48 there begins a chapter entitled 'The Town in general, its Castle, and the Capital House of Barton, Fowler and Lambard'. Dealing first with the castle, Browne Willis translates a 1632 inquisition post mortem of William Lambert, who owned the site of the Castle as well as his house in West Street. Here Browne Willis uses the phrase 'Castle House in Buckingham' to mean *the house on the site of the Castle*. In other words, Browne Willis's 'Castle House' was *not* 'our' Castle House. There was indeed a substantial house on the Castle Hill, shown on John Speed's map of 1610. It probably escaped destruction in the 1725 fire of Buckingham, but it was later rebuilt and is now called Hill House. Browne Willis states that this house 'is now (1735) the property of the family of Bridges'. This statement is confirmed by a reference in the deeds to Castle Hill. Buckingham's new church was built in 1777 on land given by Earl Verney, who had in turn purchased Castle Hill from George Bridger. Browne Willis then gives 'an account of the Capital House of Fowler and Lambard' and identifies 'Mathias Rogers, the present possessor, Anno 1735'. Browne Willis was not to know that his very clear distinction between the house on Castle Hill and the house of the Fowlers and Lamberts in West Street would later become blurred because a successor to Mathias Rogers decided to call his home 'Castle House'.

The brothers Samuel and Daniel Lysons, whose *Magna Britannia* appeared between 1806 and 1813, devoted a chapter to Buckingham. Following Browne Willis, they correctly separated their account of the castle from that of the 'capital mansion in the town of Buckingham, called Fowlers and Lambards … now the property of Mr Box'.

The element of confusion surrounding Castle House begins with George Lipscomb, whose monumental *History and Antiquities of the County of Buckingham* was published in parts between 1831 and 1847. Although there is much merit in Lipscomb's book, it does contain a large number of inaccuracies. Lipscomb takes most of his account of the Bartons, Fowlers and Lamberts from Browne Willis. Although he must have visited Buckingham many times, Lipscomb is thoroughly confused about the geography of the town. He states that 'The manorial house of Lambert and Fowler, called also Castle House, is situated a little north of the castle near the churchyard, and remained standing until modern days.' Is Lipscomb confusing the Fowlers' or the Lamberts' house with the Prebendal House, which stood just *south* of the old churchyard and was destroyed during the Civil War? Or is he confusing it with the house on Church Street, now called the 'Manor House'? This house was certainly standing in his day and was then being used by the Duke of Buckingham to hold the manor courts of his newly acquired manor of the Prebend End of Buckingham and Gawcott. Is Lipscomb confusing it with what we now call 'Hill House', on Elm Street – that is the 'old' Castle House, which then belonged to a branch of the Box family and is indeed 'a little north' of the site of the castle and of the *new* church? He would hardly have described the house we now know as 'Castle House' in West Street as being 'a little north of the castle near the churchyard'. Perhaps he had not seen any actual deeds to the Fowlers' and Lamberts' house and didn't expect it to be in West Street. Nevertheless, what we now call 'Castle House' was in Lipscomb's time and is still today the largest house in Buckingham. If it had been known by the name 'Castle House' in Lipscomb's day, he would hardly have made such an elementary mistake.

The Rev. Thomas Silvester was the Curate of Buckingham church in Lipscomb's time and was himself a historian. It is likely that the two men knew each other. Silvester has several paragraphs on West Street in his manuscript history of Buckingham, begun in 1829.[1] He commences at the *Cobham Arms*, describes the former *Cross Keys Inn*, and includes a drawing of an old house belonging to Mr Potter, a little further down the street, which he says was repaired in 1835. In a later addition he says that the same building was pulled down in 1842. This was probably on the site of the present day nursing home called 'Hamilton House'. Silvester then says that 'at the bottom of West Street on the same side is a fine old mansion called Castle House, which in the reign of Richard II was the seat of John Barton, who represented the County in Parliament'. So it seems that 'our' Castle House, only acquired its name around 1842 – perhaps even a little later, when Silvester completed his work.

But the element of confusion introduced by Lipscomb has been compounded by a further error made by a more recent historian, E.M. Elvey. Here the confusion is not between the modern Castle House and Hill House, but between Castle House and a house in the middle of Buckingham. Lacking the confidence and proximity to events enjoyed by Browne Willis, Mrs Elvey confuses documents relating to Castle House with those of another significant Buckingham house, 1-2 Market Hill.[2] When this building was demolished in 1967, elaborate wall paintings were found dating from the Tudor period. Contemporary deeds to neighbouring houses on Market Hill identified successive members of the Fowler family as owners of this property. The occurrence of the initials 'I.L.' in the frieze above the wall paintings seemed to confirm that the Lamberts had succeeded the Fowlers as owners of the house. Excited by her discoveries, E.M. Elvey concluded that 1-2 Market Hill was 'Fowlers' and that Browne Willis was wrong to identify 'Fowlers' with 'Castle House'. In fact, Brown Willis did no such thing. He was aware of the title to the Castle Hill, and the house on it, and must have seen the 1591 conveyance of Fowlers Farm which clearly states that it was in 'West Street, alias Fowlers Street'. Mrs Elvey, unfortunately, did not refer to the 1591 deed. 1-2 Market Hill never approached Castle House in size or splendour and would not have been the principal home of such wealthy and significant families as the Bartons, Fowlers and Lamberts. In particular, Mrs Elvey concludes that when Catherine of Aragon visited Buckingham in 1513, she must have stayed at 1-2 Market Hill, rather than at Castle House. In fact, a royal visit to 'our' Castle House, the 'real' Fowlers, is much more likely.

So when did 'Fowlers' or 'Lamberts' become 'Castle House'? As we have seen, a date in the 1840s seems the most likely – although it is just possible that it could have been a little earlier. When the property was sold by the heirs of Mathias Rogers in 1782, it was described as 'all that capital messuage or tenement situate lying and being in the Town of Buckingham aforesaid in a certain street there called West Street alias Fowlers Street'.[3] In 1798 the house was put up for sale by the then owner, Thomas Shillingford. The printed sale particulars do not name the house, but describe it simply as 'a Capital Freehold Mansion House ... situate in (and much detached from) the Town of Buckingham'.[4] The new owner, Philip Box, the proprietor of Buckingham's first bank, could have given the house a name. As early as 1791 he had bought the properties on Castle Hill, adjacent to the new church, from the trustees of Earl Verney. Having bought Castle House in 1798, it is possible that he borrowed the name from the first purchase and applied it to the second. Yet, in his very lengthy will of 1811, Philip Box does not name the house, simply leaving his 'capital messuage' to his nephew, also Philip Box. This Philip Box lived in the town of Carlow in Ireland and probably leased the house or even left it empty. He is unlikely to have given it its new name. His English cousin, yet another Philip Box, was an estate agent, resident at Radclive. He seems to have been involved in the sale of the house in 1837. Was it the estate agent who thought it would make the house more saleable if it had a grand name?

The first owner definitely to use the name 'Castle House' was Thomas Hearn, the Buckingham solicitor who bought the property from the Box family in 1837. He too became a partner in the local bank and was sufficiently upwardly mobile to need a house name. After all, his partner in the bank and near neighbour, George Parrott, had called his new house, off Stowe Avenue, 'Castle Farm'. The first official mention of the name 'Castle House' traced so far is in the enumerator's book for the 1851 census – that is in Hearn's time.

In thinking of Thomas Hearn, we imagine a man with social pretensions, a man with ideas above his station. The names of houses and of people can be misleading. We recall Lady Salisbury's comment when she heard that Mr Asquith intended to take the title of Earl of Oxford: 'That would be like calling a suburban villa Versailles.' Thomas Hearn was sufficiently unself-conscious to shrug off the inevitable criticism that everyone knew where Buckingham Castle was, and it wasn't in West Street. And he had the wealth and authority to ensure that tradesmen, clients, family and friends would all use the new name. He was able to say that his was *the* Castle House. We have seen what confusion can arise when two or more houses in one town share the same name.

Shakespeare was right. Names do matter.

Chapter One

LOCATION, LOCATION, LOCATION

CASTLE HOUSE is so much larger than any other private house in Buckingham that we must ask whether it was built purely as a house. Its size suggests at least a farmhouse, more likely a merchant's house, or even an institution. There has certainly been farmland attached to Castle House over the centuries. But the early owners, the Bartons and the Fowlers, made their fortunes from the law, or from lucrative positions in the City or at Court. They accumulated land in the town as an investment and had little intention of farming it themselves. According to the evidence given in Adams v. Lambert, John Barton, the founder of the almshouses in Church Street, who died in 1431, had a tenant, William Brampton, farming his land. A later owner of Castle House was Richard Fowler, Chancellor of the Duchy of Lancaster. He had extensive farmlands in several parishes around Buckingham, but Castle House would be reserved as his occasional residence in his native town, and is unlikely to have been the home farm. Later members of the Fowler family, however, had even grander country houses in Oxfordshire and Bedfordshire, and it may well be that Castle House, or 'Fowlers Farm' as it became known, did for a time lose its status and become a tenanted farmhouse. It was certainly called 'Fowlers Farm' when it was sold to John Lambert in 1591, but the term 'Farm' could possibly mean *a rented property* rather than a centre of husbandry. The Lamberts were a little nearer to the land, having started out as butchers. John Lambert, however, was already calling himself a gentleman by the time he acquired Castle House in 1591. His cousin, Simon Lambert of Buckingham, who died in 1618, also called himself a gentleman. He had a farm in Maids Moreton extending to 'four yard lands' (about 120 acres) and bought the right to collect the tithes of the Castle Hill and the Borough of Buckingham from Sir Robert Brett in 1613.[1] Both these men could be described as gentleman farmers.

Sir Edward Richardson, who married John Lambert's grand-daughter, the heiress of Castle House, was also a gentleman farmer. In his will of 1637, he referred to 'all my horses beasts sheep corn and hay either going or growing upon my grounds or in my barns either in Buckingham or Moreton'.[2] The outbuildings attached to the house in the 18th century would certainly have supported farming activity. The 1757 insurance policy for Castle House included a great barn, stone and thatched, valued at £50 and a brick and stone malthouse with tiled roof, valued at £300. (see page 69) Throughout the 19th century, Castle House belonged to professional men, so any surviving farm buildings may have been converted or removed.

So while Castle House did have the facilities required by a farmer in a large way, it was probably never a farm house – except perhaps in the 1570s and '80s. We might do better to see it as a merchant's house. It was certainly large enough to accommodate a wealthy proprietor, his family and his servants. There would also have been ample room for apprentices, and several cottages among the outbuildings to accommodate journeymen. Indeed, the extensive cellarage under the west wing, and the even deeper and more capacious cellar under the east wing, could have kept huge quantities of provisions, liquors or other saleable goods safe and cool.

Yet if Castle House was a merchant's house, it was in a strange position in relation to the town of Buckingham. Anyone who was first and foremost a merchant would not have chosen to live there. Traditionally, merchants liked to live close to their business, over or next to their warehouse. That was the best protection against burglars and fires. A Buckingham merchant or commercial man would probably have preferred to live in the centre of town – as the Lamberts did before they moved to Castle House – while successful tanners like the Bartletts would live on Hunter Street in front of the tanning pits filled with water from the Ouse. The location of Castle House has neither commercial nor manufacturing logic. For most of its existence it has been on the very edge of Buckingham, the first house travellers would have seen when they arrived from Brackley. It is striking that, apart from the 18th-century toll-house and the Militia Barracks, most of the buildings near to Castle House date only from the 20th century. In other words, therefore, Castle House marked the frontier between Buckingham and the open countryside.

Although just in Buckingham, it is really more of a country house than a town house. Its 'country role' is highlighted in the Sale Catalogue of 1903:

> This compact little Estate of Castle House including as it does sufficient good old turf land to enable a purchaser to enjoy the pastoral pursuits of Dairying, Horsebreeding etc. while the district affords the best of Foxhunting and mixed shooting and fishing is obtainable.[3]

If the building is not suitable for a farmhouse, and its position is not appropriate for a merchant's house, does that mean that Castle House had another purpose? Perhaps the most intriguing possibility is that it had a 'pre-history' as an institution, something like the Hospital of St John the Baptist in the centre of the town, now called the Chantry Chapel. There was another hospital in Buckingham, the Hospital of St Lawrence, probably founded in the 12th century for the purpose of sheltering lepers. In 1227 one Richard Blanning fell from his horse and was drowned in the River Ouse at Buckingham. The horse, however, survived the accident and was valued at three shillings. The money was given to the Hospital of St Lawrence.[4] In 1321 the master and brethren of St Lawrence Hospital were given special licence by the Bishop of Lincoln to appeal to the populace of the neighbourhood to contribute to the hospital's running costs. In 1347 one Gilbert de Buckingham gave land valued at 10 marks to the hospital 'out of compassion for the poverty of the master and brethren'.[5] There is no further information on the hospital, which may have ceased to operate after the Black Death. The site of this hospital has not been identified, but it would, like Castle House, have been a substantial building, somewhat separated from the town. Like Castle House, it would have had good cellars. The hospital would have needed extensive storage for provisions to see the master, brethren and patients through the long winters. It is a strong possibility that the redundant hospital buildings could have been converted into a private house by a wealthy Buckingham resident. In other words, the 'pre-history' of Castle House may have been as a leper hospital. Indeed, this possibility is strengthened by the fact that – as at Brackley and Banbury – leper hospitals were usually located on the edge of a town.

It really does not take much thinking to appreciate that Castle House occupies an ideal site for either an institution or a superior residence. As we have seen it is on the edge of Buckingham, it presents both an 'urban' and a 'country' face. It is adjacent to open country yet barely a couple of hundred yards from the centre of Buckingham. A 15th-century 'estate agent' would surely have said that anyone who bought the Castle House site would be able to enjoy all of the advantages of life in the country and in the town – exactly the line in 1903. We should also remember that Castle House is on the north side of the river. It is south-facing and hence the house and its gardens get more sun than houses on the other side of the Ouse. But there is more to it than that. There are several places in Buckingham where property along the Ouse is liable to flooding – in Hunter Street and in Well Street. That is likely to have been a problem for Castle House's chief 'rival', the alternative focus of authority once the Castle had gone, the Prebendal House. But the Castle House site is sufficiently far from and above the river for there to be little danger of flooding. That meant that it would be safe to construct cellars – essential for the storage of things like beer needing a cool temperature.

The West End

We should remember that the Castle House site is on the western edge of Buckingham. That too was a great advantage. In most towns in Britain, rich people tend to live in the west and poor people in the east. London provides the best example; a television 'soap' called 'West Enders' would have a very different social tone to the well-known 'East Enders'. 'West' is smart and 'east' is poor or common. Why? The prevailing wind in this country blows from the west. If you live in the east end of a town all of the smoke and fumes it produces comes your way. If you live in the west the air will be clearer and cleaner. Although Buckingham is much smaller than London, the same is true here too. The tan yards probably produced some very unpleasant smells and other trades could be pretty noisome as well. Apart from those comparatively rare times when the wind was in the east, the residents of Castle House would be unaffected. At least until the mid-19th-century, many people believed that bad smells were a major cause of disease. Thus Castle House had what appeared to be the healthiest location in Buckingham.

But the advantages of west over east are even greater when the river also flows from west to east – as the Thames does in London and the Ouse in Buckingham. Although most of the water was probably taken from wells, on occasion it might be necessary to take water from the river. The water flowing near to Castle House would have been much cleaner than after it had flowed through Buckingham. Rivers were often little more than common sewers. Downstream, especially in hot dry summers, the stench would have been awful. Of course the residents of Castle House would have contributed to the stench, but they would not be the ones who suffered from it. The advantages of west over east might seem fairly trivial in a small town like Buckingham. Buckingham people may not have even appreciated them. But, some of the eventual purchasers of Castle House were not Buckingham people. They would have been only too familiar with a highly polluted city and all that implied. As they viewed the property and the town, they would surely have appreciated that Buckingham was really a kind of miniature London. What was true of London was also true of Buckingham. They must have said 'West End every time'. In other words, the advantages of the Castle House site as the best place to live in Buckingham would have been especially obvious to anyone with experience of London. It is surely no coincidence that the first known owner was a London lawyer and that many of the subsequent Castle House families have also had links with London.

Chapter Two

FARMERS AND LAWYERS

ABOUT THE YEAR 914 King Edward the Elder built a castle at Buckingham, as part of his successful campaign against the Danes. The makeshift fortifications probably soon fell into disuse. By 1086 Buckingham was the county town of Buckinghamshire with a castle, a church and 52 burgesses. William the Conqueror gave this manor of Buckingham, along with other land in the county and elsewhere in England, to his cousin, Walter Giffard. Giffard may well have rebuilt the castle. The manor of Buckingham, with its castle, descended from the Giffards to Richard de Clare. De Clare gave the manor of Buckingham as a dowry when his daughter married William de Braose. By 1305, on the death of Giles de Braose, Buckingham Castle must have been abandoned again, for it is listed as being worth nothing.[1] Some of the de Braose lands in Buckingham were acquired by a man named William Goddes. In 1385 Goddes sold six acres of land in Buckingham to William Barton. This was the first of many such purchases by the Bartons, who accumulated a large portfolio of land in

3   Castle House, west wing, 2005.

Buckingham and the surrounding district. Their holdings eventually included a belt of land on the north side of West Street on which the house later to be called Castle House was built.

Looking at Castle House from the street, we might imagine it was built in the early 18th century. Behind the street front, however, there are two wings of Castle House which are much older. These are what the architectural historians now term 'first floor hall houses'. The ground floors of these structures were generally made of brick or stone, whilst the first floor and roof were usually timber-framed. At Castle House, the west-facing gothic windows on the ground floor of the west wing are clearly part of a stone wall, whereas the windows above are of wood and fit into the timber frame of the first floor. First-floor hall houses had domestic offices on the ground floor, but the principal family room was on the first floor, open to the roof, where elaborately

4   Castle House, east wing, 2005.

carved roof trusses were part of the decoration. The east wing is another first-floor hall house, of slightly smaller dimensions, but with more modestly carved roof trusses which were nevertheless meant to be seen. The join between the masonry ground floor wall and the timber-framed first floor can be seen as a step in the rendering of the east wall of the east wing. Both the west and east wings at Castle House have good cellarage, but the huge cellar in the east wing is unusually deep and runs the length of the house. It was lit by widows set at ground level in the west wall, each within a deep recess in the wall to allow light into the depth of the room.

Our earliest visual reference to buildings on the Castle House site is on John Speed's map of 1610; there we see a large house of some six gables surrounded by large gardens. The west and east wings could be represented by the extreme west and east gables, or they could be behind the gabled south front depicted by Speed. Castle House was then the second biggest house in Buckingham, but Speed does not name it on his map. He does name the larger Prebendal House (Speed's R). But no other house in Buckingham is in the same league and, in any case, the Prebendal House, then belonging to Alexander Denton, was to be destroyed in the Civil War – probably in 1644, at the same time as Denton's house at Hillesden. Thereafter Castle House was to have no serious competitor in Buckingham town. But how far can we trace Castle House back in time?

We just do not know if this 15th-century house was an entirely new building or incorporated parts of an earlier structure; either is possible. At any rate, we are back to the time of the Castle, or close to it. It could be that building materials from the ruined Castle were 'recycled' when new houses were built. Of course, this is speculation and it is probably wise to confine ourselves to the known 15th-century origins. What sort of society are we dealing with? In its later years, Castle House

5   Castle House, the roof timbers in the west wing, 2005.

6   Castle House, detail of roof timbers, west wing, 2005.

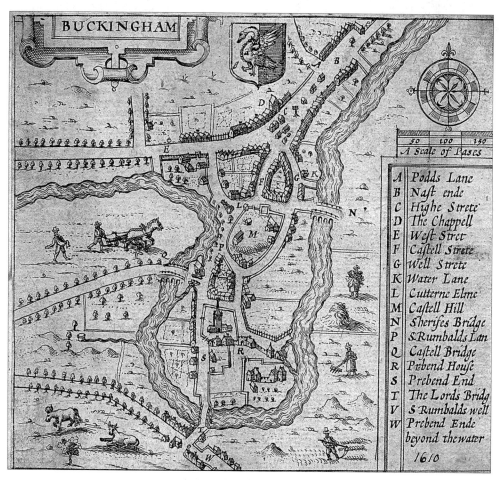

7   Speed's Map of Buckingham, 1610.

seems to exude calm and serenity, but there can be no doubt that it was 'born' in an
age of crisis and dramatic social and economic change. The land market was becoming
more fluid, offering opportunities for 'new men' of non-noble backgrounds to secure
a small estate. Their money was likely to come from essentially non-agricultural
sources. They might want some land, but probably more for the status it conferred
than for any economic reason. They would not want the land to lose money, but,
at least for the moment, it was not their chief source of income. Above all, they
wanted an appropriate residence, a seat, to provide the basis of the dynasties they
intended to establish. If they could find the right spot they were more than willing
to remodel any existing property to fit their ideas of grandeur.

The Bartons

The Bartons – the name means 'barley enclosure' – were certainly rising in the
world and could be regarded as 'new men'. Whether or not there had already been
earlier buildings on the West Street site, there had never been a manor house as
such. Indeed, although it may have resembled a manor house in appearance, Castle
House itself was never to be one in the technical sense of the word. In this respect
it was unlike the Prebendal House, Lenborough Manor or Bourton Manor. It would
not have been impossible for William Barton to acquire a house with manorial
rights attached; as we shall see, one of his sons was to do so in a village close to
Buckingham. We have to face the possibility that he was just not interested. Perhaps
he appreciated that, even in the late 14th century, manorial rights were not what
they had been before the Great Pestilence and could easily prove more trouble than
they were worth. His decision to acquire a non-manorial site may reflect a decidedly
'modern' and business-like outlook.

But if William Barton was a new man, he was probably no stranger to the
Buckingham area. In this he conformed to a broader pattern; a man of relatively
humble origins would leave his native village, go to London, make his fortune and
then return to his old home as a figure or importance and substance. No doubt he
positively revelled in the envy of his less adventurous contemporaries. The Bartons
probably originated in this area. The village of Barton Hartshorn lies only a few
miles away from Buckingham and the Bartons may have taken their name from it.
In the 14th century there were Barton families at Barton Hartshorn, at Addington
and at Thornton. One William Barton ran a small school at Thornton, and in 1388
complained to the Manor Court of Water Eaton and Bletchley that Galfridus atte
Hall had not paid the 18d. school fees due for teaching his son.[2]

William Barton

The other William Barton, the man who purchased Goddes' property in Buckingham,
was rather grander. Born in 1338, he was appointed a Coroner for Buckinghamshire
in 1377-8 and he was also a Justice of the Peace. William Barton certainly had a
very busy year as Coroner. There were two Coroners for Buckinghamshire and
Barton was responsible for the Northern Hundreds. On 26 July 1377 – a Sunday
– he held an inquest at Haddenham following the discovery of the body of Adam
Machon. The inquest decided that Roger de Bours had met Machon on Cuddington
Heath on the afternoon of Friday 24 July. Bours had struck Machon on the head
with a sword. Machon had managed to struggle home but subsequently died. The

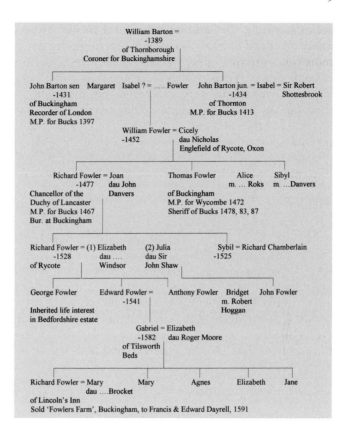

William Barton =
-1389
of Thornborough
Coroner for Buckinghamshire

John Barton sen   Margaret   Isabel ? = ... Fowler   John Barton jun. = Isabel = Sir Robert
-1431   -1434   Shottesbrook
of Buckingham   of Thornton
Recorder of London   M.P. for Bucks 1413
M.P. for Bucks 1397

William Fowler = Cicely
-1452   dau Nicholas
               Englefield of Rycote, Oxon

Richard Fowler = Joan   Thomas Fowler   Alice   Sibyl
-1477   dau John   m. ... Roks m. ...Danvers
Chancellor of the Danvers   of Buckingham
Duchy of Lancaster   M.P. for Wycombe 1472
M.P. for Bucks 1467   Sheriff of Bucks 1478, 83, 87
Bur. at Buckingham

Richard Fowler = (1) Elizabeth   (2) Julia   Sybil = Richard Chamberlain
-1528   dau ....   dau Sir   -1525
of Rycote   Windsor   John Shaw

George Fowler   Edward Fowler =   Anthony Fowler   Bridget   John Fowler
-1541   m. Robert
Inherited life interest   Hoggan
in Bedfordshire estate

Gabriel = Elizabeth
-1582   dau Roger Moore
of Tilsworth
Beds

Richard Fowler = Mary   Mary   Agnes   Elizabeth   Jane
dau ....Brocket
of Lincoln's Inn
Sold 'Fowlers Farm', Buckingham, to Francis & Edward Dayrell, 1591

8   Family tree of Barton and Fowler.

Sheriff, John Olney, was ordered to find Bours and arrest him. In September, Barton attended inquests involving murders on two successive days. On 22 September he was at Bierton attending the inquest on Gregory Welsheman who, it was decided, had been killed by William Bampton; he had been stabbed in the back with a knife called a 'thwetul'. Bampton had fled to Bierton church to claim sanctuary and now 'abjured' the realm. On 23 September Barton was at Wycombe to investigate the case of William Stevens, who had been killed by Walter Keller, using a 'baselard'. On 17 November there was an inquest on a murder at Nether Winchendon and on 14 March, on one at Olney. Perhaps most shocking was the inquest at Great Loughton, held on 4 July 1378: William Sapcote, priest of Little Loughton, had been killed by an arrow shot by John Gereyes, priest of Great Loughton. Of course there were other sad deaths – men who had fallen from ladders, or into a stream, a child run over by a cart, or poor little Agnes Thornborough of Buckingham, aged one year, who had fallen into the fire of her father's house. All in all it must have been a busy year for Barton. It has sometimes been suggested that service for a year as Coroner was a kind of 'entry ticket' to county society. For William Barton, the price of entry, in terms of time and perhaps personal distress, must have been quite high.[3]

William Barton was steward to Richard de Molyns and was himself quite a large landowner. He died on Sunday 11 July 1389 and left his estates to his two sons, both, confusingly, named John. The two Johns erected a memorial to their father in Thornborough church – a stone slab with brass figures. There is William wearing a long gown and a hood and his wife in a long cloak with a veil head-dress. A Latin inscription reads:

> Here lieth William Barton who died on the Feast of St Benedict, Abbot, in the year of our Lord 1389 and the beginning of the year of the thirteenth year of the reign of king Richard the second, when Sunday fell on the letter C, at the hour of Vespers, upon whose soul may God have mercy.
> Amen.

Nearby there is an undated memorial window which includes the Barton arms and is dedicated to William and his wife Emmote. In heraldic terms, the Barton arms are: Ermine on a Dexter. Canton Gules, an Owl Argent. The close family relationship between the Bartons and their successors at Castle House is indicated by the fact that an owl also figures prominently in the Fowlers' arms. Traditionally, the owl is associated with wisdom – perhaps both the Bartons and the Fowlers wanted to stress their links with learning and with the law.

The two John Bartons

The two John Bartons, known as John senior and John junior respectively, were educated at Oxford and became extremely successful. It is possible that John senior was in minor holy orders; in 1390 a man of this name became rector of Foscott on the presentation of Alan Ayette.[4] Yet this could have been another John Barton and it is clear that John senior's life was essentially that of a layman. He was Knight of the Shire for Buckinghamshire in 1397, 1401, 1404 and 1408.[5] In 1399 John Barton senior became Attorney to the Duke of Exeter.[6] He was later appointed Recorder of London.[7] He also continued his father's connection with the wealthy Molyns family, by becoming lawyer for Sir William Molyns.[8] John senior purchased various properties in and around Buckingham, including Addington, Foscott, Stone Manor and town houses in Buckingham and Oxford. He also had the use of two houses

9   Brass of William Barton, Thornborough Church, 1389.

in London.[9] In 1424 he purchased Skirretts Manor, in Buckingham, from John de Bekeswelle, heir of Joan Cuele, daughter of Roger Skirrett of Buckingham. The property comprised lands, rents and reversions in Buckingham, Bourton and Gawcott, and probably included the site of Castle House.[10] John Barton senior attended the procession and mass to celebrate the victory at Agincourt, held in the Guildhall Chapel on 13 October 1415. Others attending included the Mayor, Richard (Dick) Whityngtone, Robert Chichele, William Chichele and another probable relative, Henry Barton (Mayor of London, 1417).

John junior followed his brother into Parliament and was Knight of the Shire in 1413 and 1423.[11] John junior often joined his brother in land purchases and deals. All in all, they bought some twelve local manors including Stewkley. In 1418 John junior bought the manor of Thornton from the impoverished Chastillon family. The Bartons set a pattern for the owners of Castle House that has continued down the centuries. Although often away on business, sometimes going overseas, there was never anything of the absentee landlord about them. Like many of their successors at Castle House, they were actively involved in the life of the town and acutely aware that wealth brings not only privilege but also serious social responsibilities. Both were deeply religious men, concerned and alarmed at the rise of Lollardy. They were also linked with the Mercers Company, a City Company with many charitable activities, especially in the area of education. In 1422 John senior gave 200 marks to the master and brethren of the Hospital of St Thomas Acon for their relief and an annual rental of seven marks from some of his London property. The Hospital of St Thomas Acon was the Mercers' Church. Barton stipulated that the hospital was to provide a permanent chantry priest in London to say prayers for his soul and the souls of his parents.

The Will of John Barton senior

John Barton senior's will, dated 5 June 1431, is an important document in the history of Buckingham. His first concern was for his own salvation. He asked to be buried in St Rumbold's aisle in Buckingham church and allocated 40 shillings for a marble tombstone. Barton gave £16 13s. 4d. for a priest to say 4,000 masses for his soul. He gave 40s. to the master and brethren of the Hospital of St Thomas of Acon, and 40s. to the master and brethren of the Hospital of St Bartholomew, both in London. He gave 40s. to the Abbot and Convent of Biddlesden, 100s. to the Prior and Convent of Luffield, 40s. to the Prior and Convent of Chetwode and 40s. to the Prior and Convent of Snelshall, all in Buckinghamshire. He also made bequests to the Friars Mendicants of Northampton, the Friars Mendicants of Oxford, and to the Friary of Aylesbury.

John Barton left the following property in Buckingham:

> I give and bequeath to John Barton the younger my brother all my tenements, together with all the tenements which were late Roger Skiret's, which I purchased, with the rents and services, together with the reversion and all their appurtenances in the town of Buckingham, to have and to hold all the tenements aforesaid with their appurtenances to the aforesaid John my brother.[12]

John Barton junior was to inherit on condition that he found a fit chaplain – that is the one sent by the Hospital of St Thomas Acon – to say daily mass for John senior's soul and those of his father, brothers, sisters, benefactors and friends and all other departed faithful souls. These masses were to be celebrated at St James's altar in Buckingham church and the chaplain was to attend matins and vespers in the choir on all festivals. He was to read through all of the psalms every week. He could have a maximum of fifteen days' annual leave but was to find a substitute during this period. For every day he neglected to say mass he was to pay one penny to be given to some poor person in Buckingham. John Barton junior was also to find six poor men and women to pray for his soul for four pence a week and provide each with a mansion. This is the origin of the still surviving Barton's Hospital or Almshouses in Church Street, Buckingham.

The Hospital of St Thomas Acon now had two priests effectively on assignment to Buckingham – one at Barton's Chantry and the other at Matthew Stratton's Chantry – now the Chantry Chapel. The order of St Thomas Acon was much concerned with education and schools and, at this time, many schoolmasters were chantry priests. It is certainly possible that John Barton senior was the real founder of what was eventually to become the Royal Latin School, although this cannot be proved. He certainly had close dealings with schoolmasters and as early as 1423 he received a quarterly rental from the schoolmaster (*de magistro scolarum*) for his lands in Buckingham. The annual rent is one mark (13s. 4d.). As schoolmasters rarely received more than about £2 per year in the 15th century, this rental looks high and may indicate that there was some other business arrangement, perhaps involving the Hospital of St Thomas Acon.

The heavy costs of maintaining John Barton's chantry and his almshouses were charged on his Buckingham estate. The bequest of these lands to John Barton junior was for life, with remainder to his sisters, Margaret and Isabel, for their

10   Barton's Almshouses, Church Street, 1909.

lives respectively, with the remainder to William Fowler and the heirs of his body. It seems that Fowler was the son of one of Barton's sisters. If the profits of this estate were not sufficient, then Barton's executors were free to charge any further costs on his lands and tenements in Buckingham, Bourton, Gawcott, Lenborough, Maids Moreton, Thornborough, Hillesden, Water Stratford, Shalstone and Foscott, in Buckinghamshire, plus lands in Oxfordshire and a tenement in Oxford itself.

If we are to believe the account of John Barton's will given as evidence in Adams v. Lambert over 150 years later, the Buckingham estates at the time of John Barton's death were occupied by a tenant named William Brampton. But as the litigant was then trying to prove that the *revenues* of the estate had been used for 'superstitious purposes' it may well be that Brampton was tenant of the farmland rather than of Barton's house in Buckingham.[13]

John Barton junior

John Barton junior was no less rich and charitable than his brother. He derived a lucrative income from his position as steward of St Albans Abbey, which had a large estate at Winslow. Having bought the manor of Thornton in 1418, he seems to have resided there when not in London. When he died in 1434, his will directed that he should be buried in Thornton church and that a chantry priest be provided there to say mass for him and look after six poor children. In effect he set up a chantry school. Perhaps he was influenced by his brother's example at Buckingham or by Henry Chichele's establishment of a chantry school at Higham Ferrers. John Barton junior erected a memorial to his father, mother and elder brother, at the bottom of the north window in Thornton church. The memorial has since disappeared, but Browne Willis recorded it as reading: 'Orate pro bono Statu Wilhelmi Barton et Emmote, Uxoris ejus, necnon, Johannis Barton, senioris, quondam Recordatoris London. Quorum Animabus propicietur Deus'.[14] The alabaster effigies of John Barton junior and his wife Isabel also remain in Thornton church.

John junior's will was disputed by members of the Chastillon family and his widow, Isabel, became involved in complicated litigation. In order to frustrate the Chastillons, Isabel granted some of her husband's lands in Padbury (Milbury Manor), Foscott and Maids Moreton, to All Souls College, Oxford. In return All Souls agreed to pay 200 marks to Isabel and to provide three chantry priests, two at All Souls and one at Thornton, to say masses for Isabel and her late husband. To make things even more difficult for the Chastillons, the lands were first conveyed to the King and then to the Warden of All Souls.

The gift to All Souls College points to an interesting connection between the Bartons and the family of the founder of the college, Henry Chichele, Archbishop of Canterbury. By the 1440s, the Barton and Chichele families had been known to each other for more than a century. The names of both appear in Thornborough as witnesses to legal documents dating from about 1300.[15] Henry Chichele (c.1362-1443) was born at Higham Ferrers, Northamptonshire. As a boy he attended Higham Ferrers Grammar School, whose master between 1372 and 1399 was Henry Bartone. It seems highly likely that Bartone was related to the Bartons of North Bucks. He served several terms as Mayor of Higham Ferrers, alternating with Thomas Chichele, the father of the future Archbishop.[16] Henry Chichele became a protégé of William of Wykeham, Chancellor of England and founder of New College,

11 Effigy of John Barton junior, Thornton Church.

Oxford. Chichele was a Church lawyer, in close contact with lay lawyers like the Barton brothers. In 1402 the two Bartons provided a security in Chancery on behalf of Henry Chichele in a case brought against him by the Crown. Chichele became Archbishop of Canterbury in 1414, and the following year helped to secure John Barton junior's appointment as a trustee of William of Wykeham's estates. There may have been even closer family links. Eleonora Dayrell's *History of the Dayrells of Lillingstone Dayrell* notes that Florence Chichele, the Archbishop's niece, married John Dayrell in 1432. But Dayrell was her third husband; her first husband had been Sir Nicholas Peche and her second 'John Burton'.[17] It seems quite likely that 'John Burton' is a misreading of 'John Barton' and, given that John Barton senior died in 1431, his widow's remarriage in 1432 seems quite likely. When Chichele founded a hospital and secular college at Higham Ferrers, the Barton brothers were chosen as trustees.[18] In the Library of All Souls there is a 15th-century manuscript entitled *Confutatio Lollardorum*. The author is identified as John Barton and could well have been one or other of the Barton brothers. Thus we see the beginning of another long-standing link – that between the Buckingham area and All Souls. In their life times, the Bartons would have had good reason to be thankful for the friendship and support of a man as powerful as Henry Chichele. They may well have thought that, as they had been joined with him in life, so the link should be perpetuated after their deaths.

It is interesting to speculate about the nature of the Bartons' charities and the motives that lay behind them. Lawyers were extremely unpopular in the 15th century and many were corrupt. They often served the interests of great barons with little regard to justice for the poor. The Bartons may have been better than most, but there were close links between them and the grasping Neville family – the family of 'Warwick the King Maker'. Things became particularly bad as the country drifted into civil war between Yorkists and Lancastrians.

> Under cover of a dynastic struggle acts of grossest injustice were perpetrated. Judges made no pretence of impartiality, but were ready to be coerced by force or won by bribes ... Juries were ready to perjure themselves for gifts from litigants whose cases they decided, and the accounts of Abbot Wheathampstead of St Albans reveal frequent gifts to judges and sheriffs 'for favours done' in

12   Effigy of Isabel wife of John Barton junior, Thornton Church.

some lawsuit or another. The lawyer, quick to seize his opportunity, was able to demand such huge fees from his victims that the number of those entering the legal profession increased rapidly. Lawyers were genuinely hated throughout the 15th century, which confirmed the opinion of Gower that they were 'a verbose tribe' who like harlots, sold their love for money, and for whom unpleasant things were waiting in the next world.[19]

It is interesting that Vickers specifically mentions the dubious practices of St Albans Abbey – of which, as we have seen, John Barton junior was steward. It could be that the charitable gifts were signs of a guilty conscience, or perhaps they should be regarded as a kind of insurance policy for both this world and the next.

But there is more to it than that. Earlier in the Middle Ages, abbeys had received huge gifts of land and property from the laity; now a different pattern was emerging. In staying away from the great religious houses which their ancestors had favoured and endowed, the devout men and women of late medieval England were voting with their feet for something a little nearer in spirit to themselves. They found this in the parish church and the friary, the hospital and the almshouse, the chantry and the fraternity.[20] Above all, it was generosity in the face of death – the chantry – that contributed most to the heavy expenditure on church fabrics so characteristic of 15th-century England. Few of the many colleges, hospitals and almshouses would have come into existence without a memorial purpose behind them. Despite the Reformation, the Bartons were to put a distinctive late medieval stamp on Buckingham, traces of which survive to the present.

William Fowler

On the death of John Barton the younger, his estates in Buckingham, part of which were still tenanted by William Brampton, passed first to his elder sister Margaret Barton and then to the younger sister Isabel Barton. One of these sisters must have married a Fowler, for the estate ultimately descended to William Fowler, another lawyer, who had been named in the will of John Barton senior. An inventory of William Fowler's estate, taken about 1450, shows that his Buckingham property included burgage tenements in East Street, West Street, Well Street and Castle Street, and shops in 'le draperie' and 'le shoprewe'.[21] William Fowler married Cicely Englefield, daughter and co-heiress of Nicholas Englefield of Thame, in Oxfordshire.

William Fowler may have lived on his wife's estate for in 1468 he and his son Richard served on a commission to protect the land from Nether Winchendon to Waterperry from flooding by the River Thame. Another member of this commission was Richard Quartermain, Customs Officer for the Port of London and High Sheriff of Oxfordshire in 1436. Quartermain was related to the Fowlers as he had married Sibyl Englefield. In 1449 Richard Quartermain founded a chantry which survives today as Rycote Chapel, near Thame. William Fowler's son, Richard, was something of a protégé of Richard Quartermain and rose to become Chancellor of the Duchy of Lancaster. Richard and Sibyl Quartermain had no children, and Richard Fowler eventually inherited the Quartermain's Rycote property. Another son of William and Cicely Fowler, Thomas, became a lawyer and appears to have lived at Castle House in Buckingham. Thomas Fowler was MP for Wycombe in 1472 and Sheriff of Buckinghamshire in 1478, 1483 and 1487.

But lawyers themselves were by no means free of legal disputes. John Barton junior's widow, who had now married Sir Robert Shottesbrook, had to defend her title to the manor of Thornton from a branch of the Chastillon family. She was also involved in litigation with William Fowler. Fowler refused to honour his uncle's provision for the refounding of the Thornton chantry. The situation was still unresolved when William died in 1452, and Isabel in 1457. Shortly afterwards the trustees sold the manor of Thornton to Robert Ingelton, Edward IV's Chancellor of the Exchequer.

Richard Fowler, Chancellor of the Duchy of Lancaster

William Fowler's property passed to his son, Richard, a Yorkist lawyer, whose career was favoured by Edward IV, who knighted him and appointed him Chancellor of the Duchy of Lancaster. Richard Fowler was Member of Parliament for Buckinghamshire in 1467 and a Justice of the Peace for the county. It was Sir Richard Fowler who 'pulled together' the complicated legacies left by his great-uncles, John Barton senior and John Barton junior. On 8 July 1468 Edward IV granted a request from Fowler and others, including William and Robert Ingelton (who may have been relations), to implement the terms of John Barton junior's will by establishing a chantry in the Church of St Mary the Virgin, Thornton, and endowing it with lands to the value of £20 per year.

In his own will of 1477, Richard Fowler leaves to his wife Joan (Danvers) 'all the stuff of myn household in all places, and all my grayns and all my catals except my catall upon the manor of Shobendon'. She was also to enjoy 'all the revenues etc of my manor of Shobenden, Water Stratford, Stokholt, and Stuteley, Buck[ingham], Bourton, Mourton, Foscote and Shalleston, in the said County of Bucks, my dwelling place in Bucks [Buckingham] lands etc only excepted, the which I will that my brother Thomas Fowler have during life'. He also made bequests to his daughters, Sibyl Chamberlain and Joan Fowler, who was to marry Edward Stradlyng 'my ward'. There were further bequests to his sisters Alice Roks and Sibyl Danvers. A very significant bequest was to his aunt, Sibyl Quartermain. He also left 40 shillings to the churches of Thornton, Thornborough and Padbury. But Fowler's will was of greater importance for Buckingham.

Like John Barton senior, Richard Fowler also wished to be buried in St Rumbold's aisle, but ordered 'that there be no tomb, but only a flat stone laid over me, with images and escutcheons'. Again following Barton, he left money for masses and prayers for his soul and those of his family. We must presume that his wishes were respected and that he was buried at Buckingham, but in St Mary's Church, Thame there is a large tomb to Richard and Sibyl Quartermain, on which there is also a memorial brass to Richard Fowler.

The most significant part of Richard Fowler's will was, however, the provision he made for the rebuilding of St Rumbold's aisle and for a new shrine to house the relics of the child saint:

> I wolle that the aforesaid Isle of St Rumwold in the a foresaid Church prebendal of Bucks where my body and other of my Friends lyen buried the which Isle is begonne of new to be made, be fully made and performed perfitely in all things att my costs and charge: and in the same Isle that there be made anew, a tombe or shrine for the said saint where the old is now standing and that it be made curiously with marble in length and breadth as shall be thought by myn Executors most convenient, consideration had to the rome, and upon the same tombe or shrine for I will that there be sett a Coffyn or a Chest curiously wrought and gilte as it appertayneth for to lay in the bones of the said saint and this also to be doon in all things at my costs and charge.

After the rebuilding, the southern portion of St Rumbold's aisle, the great north aisle in Buckingham church, became known as Fowler's Aisle.

Given the attention to detail in his will as to the rebuilding of St Rumbold's aisle, it would be surprising if Richard Fowler did not lavish similar attention on 'his dwelling place at Bucks'. The west wing of Castle House, and particularly the elaborately carved roof timbers, may well date from this period. Indeed, the multi-gabled façade of Castle House, shown on John Speed's map of 1610, but replaced by Mathias Rogers in 1708, may have been Fowler's design. The evidence in Coke's report of the action Adams v. Lambert, that William Brampton was still the tenant of Richard Fowler's Buckingham property in 1477, must, if accurate, relate to the farmland attached to Castle House rather than to the house itself.

Richard Fowler's son, also Richard, came of age in 1485 and the trustees of his father's estate then handed to him and his wife, Elizabeth, all rights in the lands called 'Fouler's late of Richard his father'. It was in the days of this Richard Fowler that the family was to have its moment of glory.

Of course, the times of the Bartons and Fowlers had been troubled ones for the country – with the throne passing backwards and forwards between the rival houses of York and Lancaster – but, on the whole, the 15th century had been good to Buckingham. In large measure this had been due to the generosity of the Bartons and their successors. A new century was dawning – one which opened very well for the town – but which was later to bring unprecedented crisis and trauma, although later developments were never to obliterate the contributions of the Bartons and the Fowlers. Inevitably, towns with long histories are more influenced by some periods than by others. In the case of Buckingham, the impact and legacy of the 15th century is unusually strong. Buckingham's experience was somewhat unusual. In many other places, the Church appeared increasingly neglectful of its duties and faced growing unpopularity. Such communities might well respond eagerly to any prospect of

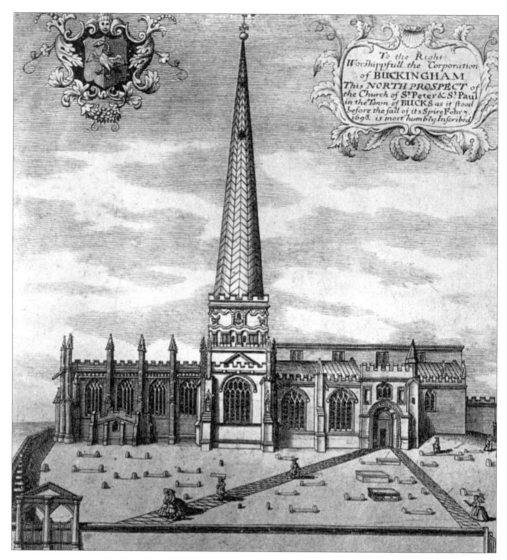

To the Right
Worſhippfull the Corporation
of BUCKINGHAM
This NORTH PROSPECT of
the Church of St Peter & St Paul
in the Town of BUCKS as it ſtood
before the fall of its Spire Febr ?.
1698. is moſt humbly Inſcribed

13   The old Church of St Peter and St Paul, Buckingham, before the collapse of the spire, 1699.

drastic changes in religion. In Buckingham, however, the town elite, represented by the Bartons and the Fowlers, together with their powerful outside patrons like Chichele, had at least tried to discharge their spiritual and social responsibilities. It is hard to escape the impression that Buckingham was content with the way things were and did not want drastic change. In view of what was to happen later, it would hardly be surprising if the 15th century assumed the aura of 'golden age'. In later centuries, Buckingham was to acquire a reputation for conservatism, for loyalty to tradition and to the old ways – in marked contrast to the 'innovations' in religion and politics favoured by its bitter rival Aylesbury. The benefactions of the Bartons and the Fowlers had surely a good deal to do with Buckingham's later character.

Chapter Three

QUEENS AND COURTS

IN THE COURSE of the 15th and early 16th centuries the Bartons and their successors, the Fowlers, established themselves as the most important regular residents of Buckingham. While retaining important contacts in London through their legal work, they were closely involved in the life of the town. Apart from quite extensive land holdings they owned a good deal of property in Buckingham itself, including some twenty burgage tenements.

Prior to the 1530s, orthodoxy and traditionalism were positive advantages. Like others of their kind, the Fowlers had faced bewildering changes of dynasty – Lancaster to York back to Lancaster and then to York and finally to Tudor. But despite their Yorkist sympathies at one stage, the family made the transition to the Tudors without any apparent difficulty. Their reputation for piety was probably an asset. Both Henry VII and Henry VIII in his earlier days saw themselves as true sons of the Church – rather more so than most of the other European rulers of their time. The early Tudors favoured people and places with similar values to their own and thus it is not surprising that Henry VII should have visited Buckingham, staying with the then young Richard Fowler in 1494.

Catherine of Aragon

Nearly twenty years later, in 1513, the Fowlers were to entertain royalty for the second time. Now their guest was Catherine of Aragon, Henry VIII's first Queen. The story of Catherine is so much bound up with the great drama of the Reformation that it is difficult to get a clear idea of her character and personality. In her last years, Catherine was a sad and lonely woman, discarded and humiliated by her husband because she had failed to give him the son he so desperately wanted. But the Catherine of 1513 was different – confident and even humorous. Later historians, especially Protestant ones, tend to portray Catherine as a symbol of Catholicism, a religion they regard as essentially un-English. Hence, they stress that Catherine herself was Spanish and foreign. They seem to forget that, over the centuries, many, perhaps most, of England's queens have come from other countries; less emphasis is placed on their foreign origins. Catherine is perceived as so 'foreign', however, that it comes as a surprise to find her staying with such a very English family as the Fowlers of Buckingham and almost certainly at Castle House. Yet Catherine was actually less 'foreign' than many of the Queens of England. It is true that she was born in Spain in 1485. A marriage was arranged between her and Prince Arthur, the eldest son of Henry VII. In 1501, aged 15, Catherine set sail from Coruna, arriving in Plymouth on 2 October. The marriage to Arthur took place in old St Paul's in

London on 14 November. But Arthur died only a few weeks later and Catherine eventually married her first husband's brother, Henry VIII. It was the question of the validity of a marriage with a deceased husband's brother that was to provide Henry with his pretext to rid himself of Catherine. But here we are concerned with chronology. Arthur died early in 1502 and Catherine did not marry Henry until 11 June 1509. In other words, she was a widow for over seven years between the ages of 16 and 23.

It is sometimes assumed that Catherine returned to Spain during these years, but she remained in England throughout. Indeed, Catherine never set foot on foreign soil between 1501 and her death on 7 January 1536. The years between 1502 and 1509 were important in Catherine's life. Queens are usually surrounded by large numbers of ladies from their own homeland and are thus 'insulated' from much contact with the people of their husband's country. During her years of widowhood, however, Catherine had few Spanish companions. She was allowed little money and often had to depend upon the charity of an increasing number of English friends. Although she never forgot her Spanish roots, Catherine learned both to speak and write excellent English – something many other 'foreign' queens never did properly. The fact that Catherine was often treated more or less as a nobody during the lifetime of Henry VII meant that she met people from a wider social circle than might have been expected. Although we cannot be certain, it is possible that she met Richard Fowler in London. In any case, we can safely say that when Catherine finally married Henry VIII, she already knew quite a lot about England and thus may be regarded as one of the least 'foreign' of England's foreign queens.

Catherine's knowledge of English ways and of English affairs is obvious in the years following her marriage. If she had been regarded as a complete outsider, would she have been entrusted with so much power and responsibility when her husband was away? Early in his reign, Henry formed an alliance with the Holy Roman Emperor, Venice and the Papacy. The alliance was directed against one of England's traditional enemies – France. In the summer of 1513 Henry joined the Emperor Maximilian on the borders of France and the Netherlands. No doubt he wanted to establish his personal reputation as a military hero; although he is often seen as a 'new monarch', Henry was still much attracted by the old ideas of chivalry. Apart from a certain amount of fighting, including the 'Battle of the Spurs' – in which Henry managed to capture a French duke – there was time enough for courtly entertainment and ceremonial. Henry thought he had achieved great things but, in reality, the campaign was unimportant. In any case the King was soon deserted by his allies and forced to make peace with France.

At home, something more serious was developing. England's other old enemy – the Scots – decided that Henry's absence from his kingdom presented them with an ideal opportunity to launch an invasion. Soon a formidable force, led by King James IV, was assembling in the Borders; in late August the Scots crossed the Tweed. The Council in London, presided over by Catherine, determined to make a vigorous response. An army, commanded by the elderly Earl of Surrey, was despatched northwards to meet the Scots. But what would happen if the Scots defeated Surrey? Military planners know that things can go wrong and that it is always wise to be prepared for this possibility. In other words, there has to be some kind of a 'fall back'. Thus, in 1513, it was decided to form a large reserve army that would assemble somewhere in the South Midlands. If Surrey's army met with disaster, there would at least be a second line of defence.

In the event, Buckingham was chosen as the point of assembly for the reserve army and Catherine left London to make the appropriate arrangements, arriving in the town on 14 September. By all accounts, it was to be a massive force. According to Garrett Mattingly: 'Along the roads that led to Buckingham levies from as far away as Wales and from all the southern and western counties were pouring to form a reserve army of sixty thousand men, which she herself [Catherine] meant to lead to York'.[1] Of course, the services of the reserve army were not needed. On 9 September 1513 Surrey inflicted a great defeat on the Scots at the Battle of Flodden Field, a battle in which King James and many Scottish noblemen were killed. A few days later a messenger arrived in Buckingham from the North bringing news of the victory. As evidence, he brought a piece of armour worn by the King of Scotland and taken from his body by the victorious English. Catherine was delighted, the reserve army was disbanded and the Queen went off to the shrine of Our Lady of Walsingham to give thanks. As far as we know, Catherine never returned to Buckingham. Although it had not been needed, we may still think the reserve army had been a wise precaution.

Sadly we know tantalisingly little of Catherine's stay in Buckingham. There are stories that she suffered a miscarriage while in the town; the stress of coping with the Scottish invasion and the uncomfortable journey on the bad roads from London to Buckingham must have been trying for a pregnant woman. But Catherine does not seem to have been sad or depressed while in Buckingham. According to one legend, before leaving she forwarded the King of Scotland's armour to Henry in France, with a slightly barbed letter in which she teased him that in exchange for his captured Duke she was sending him a King. In other words, Catherine had 'upstaged' Henry. There is no proof that such a letter was ever sent. But, if there is any truth in the legend, we see a very different Catherine to the humiliated 'Dowager Princess of Wales' of later years. In 1513 Henry was probably still in love with Catherine, but he was not a man who liked being 'upstaged' by anyone – as Thomas Wolsey was later to discover. If Catherine ever wrote to Henry in anything like these terms, she was playing a dangerous game. Could it be that the very beginnings of her matrimonial troubles can be traced to an unfortunate letter written in Buckingham at a time when her judgement was weakened by the euphoria of the news from Flodden?

While historians like Mattingly have described the events of September 1513 from a national perspective, what was their significance for Buckingham? At first sight, Buckingham seems a sensible place to collect a reserve army. It was, after all, still the county town. It was not too far from London and the drovers' roads linked it to Wales, the vital source of archers. But, on further reflection, the choice appears puzzling. A gathering point further north – Warwick, Northampton or Leicester perhaps – would have been more logical. Above all, Buckingham was too small to be suitable as the gathering point for an army of 60,000 men. It is unlikely that the Buckingham of 1513 was any bigger than the little town depicted in John Speed's map of 1610. We should remember that, if the figure of 60,000 is correct, we are dealing with a force five times bigger than the army that Charles I brought to Buckingham in 1644. How could such a tiny town provide for Catherine's huge army – if only for a few days?

If, as seems probable, Buckingham represented Catherine's personal choice, we must look for another reason. Surely the most likely explanation is that Catherine chose Buckingham as the rendezvous because she knew something of the place already, and because she had friends there. In other words, it is the very strangeness of her choice that suggests that she already knew her hosts, the Fowler family. One of the people thought to have lent or given her money during the days of her widowhood was Sir John Shaw, Lord Mayor of London in 1501. Shaw was an immensely rich Goldsmith who had been knighted by Henry VII at the Battle of Bosworth and he was also the father of Richard Fowler's second wife.

There is another reason for thinking that the Fowlers may have had had prior contact with the Queen. Of course, royal visits, however brief, can make a lasting impression on communities so favoured. Yet we still face a problem. Is Catherine's very short stay in Buckingham in September 1513 sufficient to explain what can only be described as the 'cult' of Catherine of Aragon which, the Reformation notwithstanding, was to characterise the town for centuries to come? Can it explain why Buckingham rallied so loyally to the cause of her daughter in 1553? Even more, can it explain the tradition – unlikely though it is – that it was Catherine herself who introduced the women of Buckingham to the craft of lace making? Perhaps the few momentous days in 1513 explain it all – but that seems unlikely. Is it not more probable that the Fowlers talked of Catherine before she came and after she had gone?

The Fowler Years

Historians disagree about whether Catherine's host was Richard Fowler or his son Edward. Richard Fowler is often described as 'of Rycote, Oxon', so it may have been Edward Fowler who was living at Castle House in 1513. According to the Certificate of Musters, Richard Fowler was certainly the wealthiest man in Buckingham in 1522. This document gives the annual income from lands and tenements of over thirty Buckingham landowners and the value of goods owned by a further 100 tradesmen. Richard Fowler, with declared income from land of £11 18s. 8d., is surpassed only by the Master of the Guild of St Rumbold and the Vicar of Buckingham. He also owned land bringing in £10 in the hamlet of Bourton, £9 3s. in Water Stratford, £8 in Akeley, £5 in Foscott and 16s. 8d. in Maids Moreton.[2]

Richard Fowler died in 1528. In his will, dated 10 January that year, he described himself as Richard Fowler Knight, son and heir of Richard Fowler late Chancellor of Duchy of Lancaster. He evidently spent a lot of his time in London for he left furnishings at his London home and made provision for masses to be said there if he should die in London. He also left household goods in his house at Rycote, near Thame, naming rooms such as the 'great chamber' and the 'chamber over the parlour'. He made bequests to the chapel at 'Great Ricot' and to the 'chief chantry priest of Ricot'. He left his manors of Stanbridge and Tilsworth in Bedfordshire to his eldest son George for life, with remainder to his second son Edward. He did not mention his house or property in Buckingham, but left the remainder of his estates 'within the Realm of England' to his son Edward. There was mention of a son Anthony, and of a daughter, Bridgett, wife of Robert Hoggan. There were further children by a second marriage, including John, Christopher, William, Thomas, Elizabeth and Margaret.

The manor of Tilsworth had belonged to the Chamberlain family since 1373. Richard Chamberlain, who died in 1496, married Sibyl, daughter of Sir Richard Fowler. In 1528 Sibyl's son, Edmund Chamberlain, sold the manor to his uncle, Richard Fowler. The property then passed to Edward Fowler, Gabriel Fowler and finally to Richard Fowler. In 1606 Richard Fowler sold the manor to Anthony Chester, created baronet in 1619.[3] The manor of Stanbridge (a hamlet of Leighton Buzzard) came to the Chamberlain family in 1314, and was held with Tilsworth after 1373. It passed to the Fowlers in 1528 and was sold by Richard Fowler to John Iremonger in 1601.[4] It appears that the sale of Tilsworth by Richard Chamberlain to Edmund Chamberlain was really part of a complex rearrangement of family estates; the Chamberlains actually lived at Shirburn Castle and bought it from Richard Fowler in 1527.[5]

In 1528, therefore, Castle House descended to Edward Fowler. Lipscomb notes that Edward Fowler was 'represented as a very liberal and munificent friend of the town. He was a man of great affluence'.[6] It is very likely that Edward Fowler was living at Buckingham in 1513 and was therefore the host of Catherine of Aragon. There was another royal visit to Buckingham in Edward Fowler's lifetime. Henry VIII came in 1540, but we do not know where he stayed. It may not have been with the Fowlers – who would have been seen as too closely associated with his first wife – and in any case Edward Fowler was not living in Buckingham at this time. Even in the 15th century the family is usually described as 'of Rycote, Oxon'.

Edward died on 9 September 1541. His son, Gabriel, was still a minor and in February 1542 the King granted 'custody of the body and marriage of Gabriel Fowler, son and heir of Edward Fowler, esquire, deceased' to the dead man's half brother, John Fowler, the eldest son of Richard Fowler's marriage to Julia Shaw. Edward's estates included the manors of Stanbridge and Tilsworth in Bedfordshire and the lands in Buckingham, Maids Morton, Bourton, Foscott and Shalstone.

John Fowler was an important figure in the early years of the reign of Edward VI. He was close to Admiral Seymour, an association that brought him to the Tower of London as a prisoner in January 1549 for his part in 'the lord admiral's conspiracy'. Thomas Seymour, brother of Lord Protector Somerset and of the late Queen Jane Seymour, mother of Edward VI, was extremely ambitious. He secured Fowler's appointment as Groom of the Privy Chamber and encouraged him to gain the King's confidence. Fowler was the intermediary through whom Seymour supplied the young King with money and asked for favours. It is possible that Fowler's influence over Edward was responsible for his accepting the secret marriage between Admiral Seymour and Henry VIII's widow, Katherine Parr. When Seymour felt that his influence over the King was declining, he unwisely attempted to force his way into the King's bedchamber. In the ensuing fracas, Seymour shot the King's pet dog. Seymour was eventually executed and Fowler wisely turned King's Evidence.[7] Not only did Fowler get off, but he was later appointed keeper of Petworth Park, received grants of land in Berkshire, Kent and Sussex, and represented a number of South Coast towns in the Parliaments of Edward, Mary and Elizabeth. He died in 1575.[8]

Gabriel Fowler inherited in 1557 and later married Elizabeth Moore, daughter of Roger Moore of Bicester. The couple, who lived at Tilsworth in Bedfordshire, had five children – Richard, Mary, Agnes, Elizabeth and Jane. Gabriel Fowler died on 16 August 1582 leaving his 'Parsonage of Tilsworth' to his son Richard, provided that Richard sold his 'Farm of Bucks' to provide marriage portions of £200 for each of Gabriel's four daughters. He also provided that his wife Elizabeth should have sufficient firewood for her house at Tilsworth from his wood at Blackgrove. The Fowlers seem to have been living in reduced circumstances at this time, but Gabriel was still able to make bequests to 14 servants.

The 'Farm of Bucks' was then in the tenure of Raphael Moore, probably a relation by marriage. It seems that it was Raphael Moore and his family who actually lived at Castle House at this time. The Moores were slightly below the Fowlers in terms of social status and were usually described as yeomen or merchants. Thomas Moore was named as one of the burgesses in Queen Mary's Charter of 1554 and Raphael Moore himself appears as a Trustee when Bernard Brocas leased the Borough of Buckingham to the Corporation on 26 April 1573. Given that the Fowlers had been staunch Catholics – and that their views seem to have been shared by many others in Buckingham – it would be surprising if the Moores were not of the same opinion. There are legends of a priest's hole and the skeleton and ghost of a priest at Castle House. If there is any truth in the stories they probably date from the time of the Moores. While it is true that the name More or Moore is a common one, there have been suggestions that there was a link between the Moores of Buckingham and the Catholic martyr, Sir Thomas More, whose family came originally from nearby Northamptonshire.

The End of an Era

Richard Fowler, born in 1564, was 18 at the time of his father's death. Soon after he came of age, he carried out his father's wishes and ended the Fowlers' long-standing links with Buckingham. On 11 April 1590 Richard Fowler sold his family's town properties to Raphael Moore, woollen draper, and Sylvester Stuttesburie, mercer: 'All those burgages, messuages, tenements, shops, cellars, courtyards, gardens, arable land and commodities, profits and heriditaments lying and being in Buckingham and Maids Moreton'. On 17 March 1591 Richard Fowler sold the remainder of his property in Buckingham to Francis Dayrell 'of Langport, Stowe' and to Dayrell's son and heir Edmund. The purchase price was £1050. The Dayrells acquired:

> All that scite of the manor capital messuage or chief mansion house with the appurtenances commonly called or known by the name of Fowlers Farm situate lying and being in Buckingham in the County of Bucks in the West End or West part of the said town in or near a certain street there commonly called Fowlers Street and now in the holding or occupation of one Raphaell Moore or his assignee or assignees. And all houses edifices buildings barns stables courtyards backsides gardens orchards tofts crofts several closes demesne lands arable land meadows feedings pastures commons woods underwoods waters fishings warrens rents reversions courts leet liberties franchises realties and other commodities emoluments profits and hereditaments whatsoever of what nature name or quality soever they or any of them be with all and singular their appurtenances in Buckingham aforesaid and in Gawcott Bourton Maids Moreton and Shalston in the aforesaid County of Bucks or in any of them to the foresaid scite of the said manor and to the said capital messuage or chief mansion house called Fowlers

Farm or to either or any of them belonging ... now or late in the occupation or possession of the said Raphaell Moore or of his assignees ... which said scite of the manor capital meassuage or chief mansion house and all other the above bargained premises amongst other things lately descended unto the said Richard Fowler and his heirs by right of inheritance after the death of the above named Gabriell Fowler his late father deceased.[9]

But the purchasers could not expect vacant possession. The 'chief mansion' and land in Buckingham, Gawcott, Bourton, Maids Moreton and Shalstone was 'in the holding or occupation of one Raphael Moore or his assignee or assignees'. Yet if Moore was the actual occupant, he was a sub-tenant. On 6 November 1571 Gabriel Fowler had granted a 21-year lease to Thomas Lovett commencing from the Feast of the Annunciation 1572. Thus, Moore was Lovett's tenant and the purchasers would have to wait until 1593 to take possession. There were also various charges – an unspecified rent to the 'chief lord', £7 6s. 4d. to the Crown, and £5 4s. 0d. to the poor of Buckingham. While we do not know the full extent of the property, apart from Castle House, these various 'encumbrances' – especially the remainder of Lovett's lease – probably pulled the price down. The Dayrells must have calculated that they had got a bargain; if they could only wait a couple of years until 1593 they were well placed to make a handsome profit, especially at a time when land values were rising.

Having bought Fowler's Farm on 10 March 1591, Francis Dayrell sold it to John Lambert of Buckingham on 18 June 1591. The conveyance has not been traced but it is referred to in Coke's report of the subsequent case, Adams v. Lambert.[10] It is interesting to consider whether the vendor or the purchaser got the better of the other. At the time of the sale to Dayrell, Richard Fowler, who had previously studied at Oxford, is described as 'of Lincoln's Inn'. This may suggest that Fowler was a quick-witted lawyer, not the sort of man who would sell in such disadvantageous circumstances unless he had very good reason. It seems, however, that Richard Fowler never practised as a lawyer and later accounts of him indicate that he was not very bright – a ne'er do well, a loutish and cruel man who treated his young wife abominably. It is certainly likely that Fowler was hard up in 1591 and thus the Dayrells could take advantage of his straitened circumstances. Yet not everyone thought that Fowler was stupid; as we shall see, some twelve years later he may have been guilty of an act of almost devilish cunning. Thus we cannot exclude the possibility that it was Fowler who was the clever one and that he sold the Dayrells a pup. After all, why was Gabriel Fowler anxious to advise his son to sell and hence forgo the profit that would have accrued by 1593?

In view of his family's association with Buckingham, going back to the time of William Barton, it seems strange that Gabriel Fowler wanted to end it. Perhaps the Fowlers were declining in the world; their estates had been divided several times. They may have just lost interest in Buckingham. Edward Fowler's will, dated 1541, describes him as of 'Cudysdon' (Cuddesdon), Oxon. Things may have deteriorated in Gabriel's long minority. Gabriel himself does not seem to have been a regular resident in the town. In the sale document of 1591, he is described as late of Tillerworth (Tilsworth), Bedfordshire. It is significant that when Queen Elizabeth I came to Buckingham, in 1568, she dined and rested at the Prebendal House, rather than at either of the Fowler houses. But the most likely explanation is that Gabriel and

Richard Fowler knew that their title to the Buckingham property was not entirely secure and might be challenged in the courts. The fact that Richard Fowler was a lawyer of Lincoln's Inn, even if not a very good one, makes this suspicion more plausible. Litigation would be expensive and the result uncertain. It might make more sense to sell before any claim materialised and leave the new owner to face the resulting risk, trouble and expense. Of course, it would have been to Fowler's advantage to hide this from the Dayrells.

Did the Dayrells realise they had been duped straight away? Did they sell the property to John Lambert after only three months inpossession to cut their losses? It would be hard to think of a worse time to sell – had they waited only a few months until the end of Lovett's lease, they could have expected a considerable increase in the value of the property. We can only conclude that the Dayrells panicked. Although we do not know the price Lambert paid, he would have been a fool if he had not grasped that the Dayrells were seeking to sell at a crazy time. If he had any sense, Lambert would have suspected that something was wrong and reduced his offer accordingly. Again, we cannot be certain but it would be surprising if Lambert paid more than the March 1591 price; the probability is that the Dayrells' speculation went wrong and that they lost money by it. Perhaps the secret was out by then, so that Lambert could name his own price – mentally setting aside a comfortable margin to cover any court costs.

People buy houses for all sorts of reasons. With houses, aspirations and emotions come into play and these sometimes obscure hard-headed business calculations. Lambert may have set his heart on the place – as we have seen, one of the most attractive sites in Buckingham. His family had been gradually rising in Buckingham for over 150 years and the acquisition of Castle House would prove to the world that they had finally reached the pinnacle of the town's society. Yet, in 1591, Castle House was still much the same as it had been when it was built some two hundred years earlier and in the meantime tastes had changed. Now there was much more demand for luxury and the recent tenancy by Raphael Moore, woollen-draper, indicated a comparatively lowly status. The house may have once been considered suitable for the reception of royalty, but this was clearly no longer the case. No doubt the vendors in 1591 would have given John Lambert the Tudor equivalent of the estate agent's patter: 'A wonderful property Sir, with tremendous potential. Perhaps in need of some modernisation, and hence offered at a most attractive price – and (behind his hand) for other reasons we need not go into here.' It was to be the work of the new owners, the Lamberts, to make Castle House once more fit to receive royalty.

Famous Cases

So who were the Lamberts? Like the Fowlers, they had had been connected with Buckingham for a long time. We first encounter them in 1454 when they had 'a great Corner shop in the Shambles with six shops new built and to the Great corner shop pertaining'. In other words, the Lamberts were butchers. They were leading members of the Butchers Guild and were prominent members of the Trinity Fraternity. In the late 15th and early 16th centuries, they were often witnesses, along with the Fowlers, when the Trinity properties, including the bakery in Well Street, were let to men like Thomas Ellis. The name John Lambert appears as Bailiff in 1495, a position held by John Lambert in 1548 and 1553 – the man who bravely proclaimed Mary Tudor as rightful Queen and thus gained Mary's thanks in the form of Buckingham's first charter – John Lambert in 1564 and 1582, Simon Lambert in 1595 and 1606, and Thomas Lambert in 1631.[11] Other dynasties such as the Moores, the Illings and the Millers ran the Lamberts close, but no other family provided so many bailiffs.

The Lamberts of the 17th century were not especially proud of their earlier history as Buckingham butchers. They produced an 'alternative pedigree' that traced their descent from a John Lambert of Calton, Yorkshire, who arrived in Buckingham early in the reign of Henry VIII. Although they seem to have been successful as butchers, their rise to a higher social status occurred in the days of John Lambert, father of the purchaser of Castle House. This John Lambert, Bailiff of Buckingham in 1564, married Alice, the daughter and heiress of William Muse of Oxfordshire.

The Lamberts seem to have taken over the old Fowler house in Market Hill first – probably in the 1570s or even earlier – transforming it with elaborate decoration and plasterwork. No doubt Alice's money helped. By this time they had acquired a coat of arms: 'Gules, a chrevron Or between 3 Lambs passant argent, a chief cheque Or and Azure'. The lambs clearly implied a reference to their name and perhaps to their origins as butchers. When John Lambert was buried on 13 June 1578 he was described as 'Gent, Burgess and Justice'. The Lamberts too were following the Barton and Fowler tradition of generosity to the community. When John Lambert's widow, Alice, was buried on 7 March 1586, it was noted that she had 'built the highway from Castle Lane to the Almshouses by the Church'.

Yet what was the 'secret' of Castle House? John Lambert may have known something of it already, but it probably turned out to be more complicated and expensive than he had ever guessed. Although Lambert was to live to gain undisputed possession, he was an old man by the time the struggle was over. The work of transformation that he may have contemplated had to be left to his successors. There must have been times in the long years between 1591 and 1607 when Lambert wondered whether it had all been worth it.

The best way to begin the story of the secret is to turn away from Buckingham, but only for a few miles, to the little villages of Lillingstone Lovel and Lillingstone Dayrell. In the 16th century the Dayrells were the Lords of Lillingstone Dayrell, as they had been for the past three hundred years. The 1591 purchasers of Castle House – Francis and Edward Dayrell – were members of this long established family. In nearby Lillingstone Lovel the dominant family was the Wentworths, more recent arrivals than the Dayrells.

It seems that there was little liking between the two. The Wentworths were strongly Protestant and Paul Wentworth, who represented Buckingham in the reign of Elizabeth I, was a constant thorn in the side of the Queen and her Ministers. Perhaps in an attempt to appease the Wentworths, on 24 July 1584 Elizabeth granted a patent to Sir Thomas Wentworth and his heirs and assignees to take for himself such 'lordships and Lands as were concealed or unjustly detained from Her Majesty'. The grant was to the Yorkshire branch of the Wentworth family, but they may have encouraged their relations at Lillingstone Lovel to do a little 'detective work' on their account. What could be better than if the Wentworths could 'discover' some such property that had recently been acquired by their rivals, the Dayrells? If the claim could be substantiated, Francis and Edmund Dayrell would lose part or all of their 'investment' and be left looking foolish into the bargain. Of course, the

Dayrells might find some 'sucker' to sell the property to, but even then there was surely a good chance that the purchaser would sue them in an attempt to recoup his losses. The Wentworths themselves might also expect to incur substantial costs to make good their claims, so it might be better if they too disposed of their interest for ready cash. It seems that they did so, to Edmond Downing and Robert Rant, who in turn sold to Robert Snelling and Thomas Butler.

In due course, the Queen, on the petition of Henry Lord Wentworth, granted to Theophilus Adams and Thomas Butler of London:

> Inter alia, one acre of arable land in Eaton [Water Eaton] in the occupation of Robert Foster; the chantry in the Parish of St Peter in Buckingham and all lands and tenements to the same belonging or to sustain Chaplains or Priests, or other superstitious uses in the Church of St Peter, according to the order of John Barton, sen., at the annual rent of 4d. for the land at Eaton and 13s. 4d. for Bartons Chantry.

In 1597 Adams began an action against the new owner, John Lambert. The case lasted for four years and ended with victory for Adams. In 1607, however, Lambert finally settled with Adams to become the undisputed owner. When Adams began his action in the Court of the King's Bench, Lambert is described as being 'in the custody of the marshal of the Marshalsea'.[12] In other words, Lambert, a leading citizen of Buckingham, was under arrest and perhaps in prison. Adams claimed that on 23 May 1594 he had taken a ten-year lease on a property in Buckingham known as the Conigree, together with ten acres of pasture land, from Robert Snelling gent and Thomas Butler gent. On 16 April 1597 Adams had entered the property but, the very same day:

> … the aforesaid J. Lambert … with force and arms &c. entered into the tenements aforesaid with the appurtenances upon the possession of the said Theophilus thereof, and him the said Theophilus from his farm thereof, his term aforesaid not yet ended, ejected, expelled and amoved, and from his possession thereof held out and yet holdeth out, and other wrongs to him did, against the peace of the said lady now Queen, to the damage of the said Theophilus of £20.[13]

Thus Adams entered 'a plea of trespass and ejectment of farm' against Lambert. Adams was represented by his attorney, John Povey, and Lambert by J. Harborn. It was soon clear that the basis of the dispute stretched far into the past – way before the events of April 1597. It went right back to the will of John Barton senior, dated 5 June 1431. The account of the case then prints the full text of Barton's will.[14] At that time the property in question, together with six acres of pasture, undoubtedly belonged to Barton. The tenant, probably of the land rather than the house, was William Brampton. But the crucial point was that the revenues from the estate were applied to 'to the several uses and intents in the aforesaid last will of the aforesaid John Barton the testator above expressed'.[15] Things had continued in this way for several generations. They continued through the life times of John Barton junior, his sisters Margaret and Isabel, William Fowler and Richard Fowler. At the time of Richard Fowler's death, another William Brampton was still tenant of the land. As late as 1536, it was claimed, the revenue from the property was still being applied 'to the uses, intents, and appointments in the said testament and last will declared and limited'.

In February 1536, however, an Act of Parliament was passed, described as intended 'for transferring uses into possessions'.[16] Before that time, the Fowlers and their predecessors had not been the outright owners of the property. Thus, when Edward Fowler succeeded his father, he merely 'took and had' the property. The point was that, like other landowners, John Barton senior had really created a trust, known as a use. The purpose of this had been to escape what were really the equivalent of death duties – the fines payable to the Crown when an existing owner died – and, above all, to keep the property out of wardship. As a result of the change, Fowler became 'seised of and in the aforementioned messuage and six acres of pasture'. In a sense Fowler's ownership was more secure, but it was also more vulnerable to the attention of the Crown – in the shape of wardship costs. When Gabriel Fowler inherited, the property became his – if it was his – in fee simple.

If Edward Fowler had treated the land as his own absolute property after 1536 and simply discontinued the payments to the chantry, things might have been different. But Adams insisted that the terms of Barton's will had still been honoured after 1536, as before. Everything continued as it had done since 1431. For practical purposes, the change of tenure had made no difference. Everything was changed, however, by an Act of Parliament passed in 1547, 'concerning the colleges, free chapels, chauntries, fraternities, guilds and other spiritual promotions'.[17] It was the essence of Adams' case that, as the income from the property had been used not for the Fowler family's private needs but for Barton's various religious works, it now passed to the Crown. In other words, as a result of the Act, 'the aforesaid King Edw. 6 immediately after the Feast of Easter next following, after the making of the said Act of Parliament, was seised of an in the aforesaid messuage and the aforesaid six acres of pasture'. Thereafter the property descended with the Crown – to Mary I and to Elizabeth. The Queen had been entirely within her rights to grant the property to Edmond Downing and Richard Rant. Downing and Rant disposed of the estate to Robert Snelling and Thomas Butler who in turn granted a lease to Adams. The land was then occupied by Lambert who, as we have seen ejected Adams when he sought it take it over. Thus the real issue of the case centred upon the terms of the Chantries Act.

Not surprisingly the jury found themselves totally perplexed. They declared that they were 'utterly ignorant' whether Lambert had been guilty of trespass or not.[18] The only significant advice they could give was that the charge against Lambert could only apply to the house and six acres; the other four were certainly his. Even the judges were divided but, after several hearings, the views of Sir Christopher Yelverton in favour of Adams prevailed. If anything the judgement is even more complex than the case itself. The account of the proceedings was drawn up by Sir Edward Coke, but Lord Ellesmere – certainly no friend of Coke – believed that he had made a poor job of it:

> Where in his epistle to his seventh book he would make men believe that in all his reports he had avoided obscurity and novelty … yet, whoso doth read Adams and Lambert's case shall run into a wood or thicket, out of which he shall not easily wind himself.[19]

It seems that Lambert's lawyers argued that, while John Barton senior had made very specific provision for the sums of money to be devoted to his chantry and other benefactions, he had not actually endowed them with lands and hence these could not be forfeit. Furthermore, it appeared that the King had never formally approved Barton's chantry. Thus it had no legal property of its own and thus there was nothing to confiscate. But Yelverton dismissed both arguments. He maintained that if a testator left property to members of his family, 'to procure the performance of superstitious uses', the lands themselves should have passed to the King under the terms of the Chantries Act. Even if the lands concerned produced considerably more than the sums of money mentioned in the will, sums used by John Barton junior and his successors for their own use, the land should still come to the Crown.[20] Barton's insistence that his descendants would forfeit all their rights in his estate if they failed to abide by his instructions appeared to clinch matters.[21] Above all, the whole tone of Barton's will had been to promote superstitious practices rather than to advance the interests of his legatees. Lambert might perhaps have had a case if Barton's will had placed a term on the continuation of his chantry, but he had specifically declared that the masses for his soul were 'to have continuance for ever'.[22] Even if Barton's chantry had never been legally recognised as such, the fact that he had used the word 'chantry' twice in his will meant that it came within the terms of the Act. In effect Yelverton believed that 'if it looks like a Chantry and has the reputation of a Chantry, then it is a Chantry'. In short, Yelverton was sure that 'all the land in this case was given to the King by the said Act'.[23] Numerous precedents, including those of a College at Greystock, Churches in the Diocese of David's, and Chantries attached to St Paul's Cathedral, were cited in support of the judgement. It looked as if John Lambert's plans had ended in disaster.

Around the turn of the 16th and 17th centuries, the superstitious – and most people were at the time – must have regarded Castle House as 'unlucky'. It seemed to bring misfortune to everyone connected with it – however remotely. The tribulations of John Lambert, the legal expenses and the likely spell in the Marshalsea prison, were as nothing compared to what happened to the former owner, Richard Fowler and his wife. In 1591, the same year as the sale of Castle House to the Dayrells, Richard married Mary Brocket, the niece of his step-father, Sir John Brocket. Richard was then 27 and his bride only 13. The marriage seems to have been unhappy from the start and Richard soon left to travel abroad. He was away for some four years. During his absence, Mary acquired a lover – William Haynes – although when Richard returned a reconciliation of a sort was arranged. But Richard soon resumed his old abusive ways. In 1599 a portmanteau was discovered in London containing a bottle filled with yellow powder and a letter addressed to Fowler, apparently from a correspondent in France, urging him to poison Queen Elizabeth. The material was examined by the Privy Council; Fowler was arrested and sent to the Tower of London. It seemed only too likely that Richard Fowler would soon face a traitor's death. Of course, there had been numerous plots against Elizabeth's life and the merest suspicion of treason was often enough to condemn a man. But Fowler was lucky. It soon became clear that the portmanteau was not of French origin at all but had been made in London and there were strong suspicions that the letter had been written in England. In other words, someone was trying to 'frame' Richard Fowler, someone who wanted him out of the way. The deception was so obvious that Fowler was soon released.

But who would want Richard Fowler out of the way? The people with the most obvious motives were Mary Fowler and her paramour William Haynes. It looked as if a wicked and immoral woman had chosen a particularly nasty way of ridding herself of an unwanted husband. In the event it was not Richard Fowler who was put on trial but Mary and William. The trial took place before the Star Chamber where the case against the accused was led by the Attorney General, Sir Thomas Coke – the very man who was to write up the case of Adams v. Lambert. But while Adams v. Lambert was of great technical interest, its details were hardly sensational. The case in the Star Chamber was sensational to a degree. Mary Fowler and William Haynes were found guilty and Mary was sentenced to life imprisonment.

At this distance in time it is difficult to know whether Mary was really guilty. It is possible that she was not. Perhaps it was Richard Fowler – or at least Richard Fowler's friends – who schemed to get rid of Mary. Perhaps Richard arranged to have the deliberately unconvincing evidence against himself 'planted' in the expectation that he would be arrested and released; then the suspicion would fall on his wife. If so, it was an incredibly risky strategy, but it may well have succeeded. If there is any truth in this version of events, then Castle House was well rid of Richard Fowler. Of all of the owners of Castle House, the Fowlers lasted longest – for around 150 years. Most seem to have been decent and honourable men. In some ways it is sad that the association should have ended with Richard Fowler. Even if he did not indulge in the despicable trick against his wife suggested above, Fowler was surely a most unpleasant character. But then all families, even the best, usually have a black sheep somewhere. The time had come for Castle House to move on to the care of the Lamberts – in most respects a great improvement.

Chapter Four

STUART SPLENDOUR:
COURT AND CITY

ALTHOUGH ADAMS had won his case, John Lambert was still determined to acquire Castle House. But how was this long-standing ambition to be achieved? The costs involved in Adams v. Lambert had probably been heavy and Lambert may well have concluded that further litigation would prove even more expensive and might well fail. Lambert's brother William, a former Fellow of New College, Oxford, was a distinguished lawyer, a Bencher of Lincoln's Inn and a Master in Chancery, who was appointed as Keeper of the Rolls in 1597 and of the Records in the Tower in 1600. But William died in 1601 and, without his professional advice, prospects must have looked bleak. But there was a way forward after all, one that would resolve the matter for good. In 1607 Lambert bought out Adams's claim; perhaps this is what Adams had wanted all along.

The Lamberts' property

John Lambert certainly had more than enough resources to buy Adams out. He may well have planned to use some of the remainder to begin the work of remodelling and rebuilding at Castle House. If there had been no Adams v. Lambert, it is possible that Castle House would have been rebuilt in the late-Elizabethan style. Tastes in architecture were to change dramatically from the 1590s to the 1620s. We can only speculate about what an 'Elizabethan' Castle House would have looked like, but it would surely have been very different from the Jacobean mansion created by John Lambert's son. Depending upon our taste, we may either blame or credit Theophilus Adams for the delay.

It cannot have been shortage of money that prevented John Lambert starting the work. It is important to appreciate that the purchase of Castle House represented only a fraction of the substantial estate that John Lambert built up in the course of his lifetime time. It is true that Lambert had inherited a farm at Maids Moreton from his father, but he also made several significant purchases. Lambert's will, dated 16 March 1610, refers to Graies Fields, bought from John Miller, the lease of Thorborough Grounds, bought from William Standish, and 'All my manner of Stockhold alias Stockwell with all the appurtenances in as large and ample manner as I myself bought it with all the furze thorns trees woods and underwoods there growing.'

Lambert left his wife Margery a life interest in Castle House:

> I give and bequeath to Margery Lambert my wife two bedsteads with two feather
> beds two bolsters two pillows and two pillow beares with two blankets and two
> coverlets to them belonging (but not my best coverlet which I had before I married

her) and all her linen and plate which I had with her with some convenient brass and pewter as she shall need. And I give more to the said Margery my wife during her widowed state all that my now dwelling house with all barns stables backhouses yards courts gardens orchards hovels and all such firewood as shall remain at my decease and all the two closes which are mine on the backside of my said house she repairing all the premises during her widowed state paying no rent therefore but only such chief rents as belong to the Church and Lords of the fee and so in the end of her life or widowed state she to leave the house with the aforesaid premises well and sufficiently repaired. Item I give more to my said wife Margery the stock which she now hath to trade with all and also the sum of two hundred pounds of lawful money of Great Britain.

His son John was to receive £400 one year after he had completed his apprenticeship. Lambert clearly owned another house in Buckingham. John was to inherit 'my house situated over against the Backhouse [Bakehouse] in Buckingham ... now in the occupation of one Wolfe. John was also left his father's 'stragling land' in Maids Moreton and two acres of meadow in Moreton Meades. There was a bequest of £200 to Lambert's daughter Elizabeth Every and her children and a further £100 to his daughter Alice Foxley and her children. Lambert left 10 shillings to his former servant John Harrington and 6s. 8d. to all his servants living with him at the time of his death. At the end of his will, seemingly as an afterthought, he left a further £100 each to his wife and children John, Elizabeth and Alice.

But, although Lambert made quite generous provision for his wife and younger children, the bulk of the property went to his eldest son and heir, William Lambert. William was his father's sole executor and proved the will on 17 April 1610. In addition to the reversion of Castle House and the adjoining closes, he received the farm at Maids Moreton, Graies Field, the lease of Thornborough Grounds and the manor of Stockholt. Indeed, despite the legacies to other members of the family,

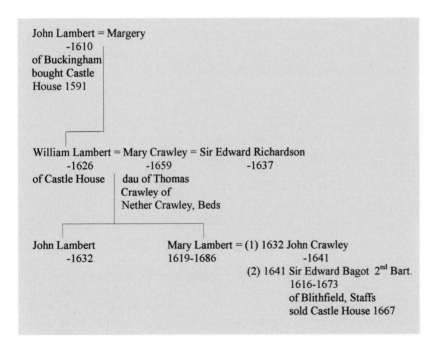

John Lambert = Margery
-1610
of Buckingham
bought Castle
House 1591

William Lambert = Mary Crawley = Sir Edward Richardson
-1626   -1659   -1637
of Castle House | dau of Thomas
                Crawley of
                Nether Crawley, Beds

John Lambert   Mary Lambert = (1) 1632 John Crawley
-1632   1619-1686   -1641
                                   (2) 1641 Sir Edward Bagot 2nd Bart.
                                   1616-1673
                                   of Blithfield, Staffs
                                   sold Castle House 1667

14   Lambert family tree.

William Lambert was now sufficiently wealthy to contemplate the rebuilding of Castle House – something his father had probably wanted to do ever since the 1590s. Indeed, it does not even seem that the costs of rebuilding put any serious strain on his finances. At much the same time that he was rebuilding Castle House, he was able to make two major additions to the substantial property portfolio he had inherited from his father. Of course, the late 16th century had seen rapid population growth and hence rising food prices and land values. It seems that the major beneficiaries were small rather than large landowners. The Lamberts, father and son, could thus represent a good example of a phenomenon much discussed by historians: 'the rise of the gentry'.

William Lambert, who thus inherited Castle House in 1610, was the son of John Lambert by his wife, the former Margaret (Margery) Perot (married 1577). He was baptised at Buckingham on 20 November 1582 and matriculated at Magdalen Hall, Oxford, on 30 July 1596. He married Mary Crawley, daughter of Thomas Crawley of Nether Crawley, Bedfordshire, and sister of Francis Crawley, 'one of the King's Justices'. [1] The most important additional properties acquired by William Lambert were the site of Buckingham Castle and the attached Castle Farm, but, as we shall see, there were others. The conveyance has not been traced, but the Castle Farm was certainly in William Lambert's ownership by 1619 for it provided the source of the water supply to the house constructed in that year.

The Defeat of the Dayrells

As we have seen, the Dayrell family, which had several branches in the area, made a 'bid' to acquire Castle House when they bought it from the Fowlers. Though of more ancient lineage than the Lamberts, they too were 'rising'. If the Dayrells had succeeded, the subsequent story of Castle House might have been rather different; it is an interesting 'might have been'. Perhaps we should see late 16th-century Buckingham as something of a battle-ground for the rival ambitions of the Lamberts and the Dayrells. Of course, the Lamberts won the 'battle for Buckingham', but although the Dayrells lost and were forced to 'retreat' to Lillingstone Dayrell, their line was to survive and retain Lillingstone Dayrell until well into the 19th century – long after the Lamberts had disappeared. In the late 16th century the Dayrells, this time represented by the branch settled at Lamport, Stowe, certainly had a powerful presence in Buckingham.

Their most significant purchase had been made in 1575, when they bought the site of Buckingham Castle, along with the Castle Mills, from the Trustees of Bernard Brocas. The castle and manor of Buckingham had formed part of the possessions of Humfrey Stafford, created Duke of Buckingham in 1444. Surviving accounts of 1473 include the cost of tiles and nails for the repair of the cook's chamber, the stables, and the garret within the castle. [2]

After the 3rd Duke of Buckingham, Edward Stafford, was executed for treason in 1521, the Castle and the manor or borough of Buckingham reverted to the Crown. In 1526 it was granted to Henry Carey, later the husband of Mary, sister of Anne Boleyn. Carey sold Buckingham in 1552 to Robert Brocas of Horton, near Edlesborough. It was Robert's son, Bernard Brocas, who split up the estate in the style of the modern asset stripper. Bourton was sold to Nicholas West in 1560. Buckingham Borough was leased for 1,000 years to the Corporation in 1572 for an

annual rent of 40s. Buckingham Castle and the farmland attached to it were sold
to Francis Dayrell of Lamport, Stowe. Camden describes Buckingham Castle about
this time as 'seated in the middle of the town upon a great mount, of the very ruins
of which scarce anything now remains'.[3] John Speed's map of 1610 shows only a
few sheds or barns on the Castle site (M).

As part of their 1575 purchase of Buckingham Castle, the Dayrells also acquired
the Castle Farm. This is referred to as early as 1279, when Buckingham Castle
appears in the Hundred Rolls, in the occupation of William de Braose, who held
with it three carucates of land in demesne and a free fishery.[4] Although the size of
a carucate varied from place to place, its normal extent was about 120 acres. In this
case, therefore, we are looking at an estate of about 360 acres. Land 'in demesne'
was usually in strips, intermixed with those of the tenants who worked on the lord's
land in lieu of rent. After the Black Death, landlords found it difficult to find any
tenants at all, let alone ones prepared to work on the lord's demesne. This land was
therefore either rented out or farmed by an agent on behalf of the lord. The agent
would need a farmhouse, a place to keep money safe before passing on to the lord
and somewhere to over-winter his cattle and to store grain.

It may be that, to begin with, the Castle itself fulfilled this role, but that would not
have been very convenient. The logical thing to do was to centre the administration
of the estate on a home farmhouse, which could serve as a residence for the lord's
steward or reeve. Such a farmhouse would have been desirable even before the Castle
fell down; afterwards it would have been imperative. We shall see later where the
agent's house was in fact located. The Castle Farm is fully described in the 1575
deed conveying the Castle Hill to Francis Dayrell:

> All that farm or tenement with the appurtenances situate and being in the parish
> of Buckingham in the County of Bucks aforesaid now or late in the occupation
> of the aforesaid Francis Dayrell or his assigns vulgarly called or known by the
> name of the Castle Farm and all and every the houses edifices barns stables
> yards orchards arable pasture and meadow woods underwoods wastes waters
> fisheries …
>
> And all those two water mills with the appurtenances in the said parish of
> Buckingham vulgarly called the Castle Mills …
>
> Four acres of Meadow or pasture in the said parish of Buckingham aforesaid
> vulgarly called or known by the name of the Mill Holmes in Buckingham aforesaid
> now or late in the occupation of James Balle or his assigns …
>
> And also all that course of water and river called Buckingham River in the
> parish of Buckingham …
>
> And also all those twenty messuages or cottages with the yards and cartilages
> adjacent lying and being in the parish of Buckingham aforesaid late in the separate
> occupations of Jastlyn Bottefish Henry Gardiner Robert Gildexter Christopher
> Glossop John Alexander John Apowell John Trobevell Catherine Lilyne Michael
> Hearing John Rawlyns Thomas Yonge John Mekyns Edward Miller Christopher
> Stafford William Phillipes Ralph Antonburie Richard Rolles … Francis Robert
> Robyns John Bristowe Edward Matheson Robert Harris Michael Hearing and
> William Gyell or their assigns.
>
> All and singular the premises with the appurtenances late were parcel of the land
> and possessions of Edward late Duke of Buckingham for high treason attained
> To hold of the Lord Queen as of her manor of East Greenwich in free and
> common socage and not in chief nor by military service.[5]

The Castle Farm, purchased by the Dayrells in 1575, was conveyed to the Lamberts some time between 1613 and 1619. In other words, the Lamberts had first 'seen off' the Dayrell challenge to Castle House – though at considerable subsequent cost – and now they moved to 'invade' more of their territory. The church tithes on this land were specifically excluded from a conveyance of the Prebendal House and manor of the Prebend End of Buckingham to Sir Thomas Denton of Hillesdaen in 1613. The tithes were then described as:

> And all the tithes of Greys Field and of the meadows thereto belonging and of the Castle Hill Castle Fields Kill Closes Gallows Close And of all the closes meadows hades pastures and hereditaments now or late the freehold or inheritance of Edmund Dayrell of Lamport in the said County of Bucks gentleman and now being in the tenure or occupation of Simon Lambert and of one John Nicholls gentleman or of their assignee or assigns.[6]

This land not only included the site of Buckingham Castle, along with about 60 acres of farmland, but also a house from which the land was farmed. This building emerges from the shadows in 1618 when Simon Lambert left a messuage in Buckingham, then in the occupation of his friend John Nicholls, and when William Lambert used it as a dowry in 1622 on the marriage of his sister, Joan Lambert, to John Nicholls of Buckingham the younger, gentleman. The property is described in a 1622 marriage settlement found in the same deed parcel as the 1575 conveyance already quoted:

> All that messuage or tenement with the appurtenances situate lying and being in Buckingham aforesaid in the said County of Bucks in a street there commonly called the West Street now in the tenure or occupation of John Nicholls the elder gentleman father of the said John Nicholls the younger or his assigns the River of Ouse being towards the south and the said street towards the north.[6]

This can be none other than the present stone-built house at the junction of West Street and School Lane, now called the Corner House and occupied for many years by Dr Bostock. A large enclosure with a house and barn appears in just this position on John Speed's map of 1610. A Mr John Nicholls was buried at Buckingham in 1646. Joan Nicholls, widow of John Nicholls, and her son, another John Nichols, were still occupying this house in 1658. They must have been living in reduced circumstances, however, for the house had by this time been divided into three tenements.[7]

The Rebuilding of Castle House

About 1617, William and Mary Lambert embarked on a substantial rebuilding programme at Castle House. The west wing, formerly a first-floor hall house, was converted into three storeys. The domestic offices on the ground floor became the great parlour, the former hall on the first floor was divided into bedrooms, complete with panelling and plastered ceiling, and the roof space became attic bedrooms. New corridors were built in the courtyard to give access to the ground- and first-floor rooms. One of the most striking features of Castle House today is the oak chimney piece which dominates the great parlour and carries the Lambert arms, the initials W.L. and M.L. and the date 1617. Lambard was careful to date his various improvements and years ranging from 1617 to 1623 can be seen in various parts of the house.

The same process must have taken place in the east wing of Castle House. Some of the datestones referred to above are in fact placed in the west wall of the east wing, facing into the courtyard of the house. The masonry around these datestones has been disturbed so they may not be in their original position. We cannot therefore be confident that the east wing was modified at exactly the same time, but it too had a new ceiling inserted above the first floor, so creating several attic rooms and concealing the decorated timbers of the roof.

The Conduit

Perhaps the most ambitious project was to bring fresh water to Castle House from St Rumbold's Well, a distance of about half a mile. The water was carried in a system of lead pipes. A new building was erected to cover St Rumbold's Well and became known as the Conduit House. The project seems to have taken a while. The pipes entering Castle House are dated 1619 but the Conduit House was not completed until 1623. The provision of a water supply of this kind was regarded as an extraordinary luxury; most similar houses of the time would have had to make do with wells or pumps in their courtyards.

William Lambard entered into an agreement with the town authorities, allowing him to carry his pipes over the Tingewick and Brackley roads. This agreement was confirmed from time to time. Thus James Harrison claimed to have seen an indenture, dated 22 January 1667, whereby:

> The Bailiffe and Burgesses of the Borough of Buckingham, for the consideration therein mentioned, did give and grant to the said Wm. Lambert, full licence and authority to continue certain pipes of lead over the highway from Castle Mills towards Tingewick and also from Fowlers End towards Ratley [Radclive] also across the River Ouse, as they were then laid, and to continue the same from St Rumbold's Well into the dwelling of the said Wm. Lambert[8]

But the conduit may have had symbolic as well as practical significance. The Dayrells had previously owned the source of the water and even aspired to Castle House itself. The conduit could be seen as a symbol of the Lamberts' victory by constituting a physical link between two properties now firmly belonging to the Lamberts but which, if things had turned out differently, could have been Dayrell territory. Of course, we do not know if William Lambert thought like that, yet the fact that he was so eager to place datestones bearing his own initials all around Castle House suggests a strong desire to 'mark' it as Lambert territory: in other words lots of Ls rather than lots of Ds.

But, despite their building works, William and Mary Lambert had much sadness. They had several sons, but most died young. William Lambert himself died on 9 August 1626 without making a will. An inquisition post mortem was held, showing that:

> He held Castle House of the king as of his manor of East Greenwich by fealty and in common socage' and 'a messuage late Fowlers with twelve acres of pastures appurtenant of the bailiff and burgesses of the Borough of Buckingham in free and common socage, by fealty and suit of court and rent of 12d[9]

The reference to 'Castle House' here is not to Lambert's house on West Street but to the Castle itself. In using the term 'Castle House', the official taking evidence

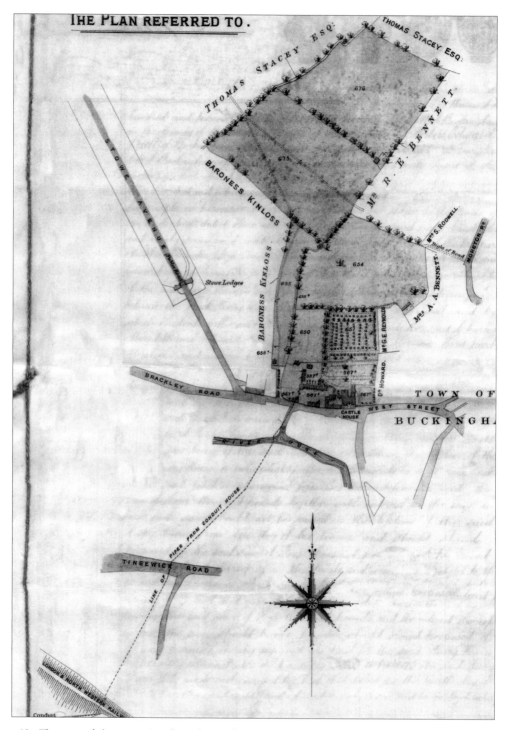

15 The route of the water pipes from the Conduit House to Castle House, as shown on a conveyance of 1904.

probably means *the house on the site of the castle*. It is held 'of the king as of his manor of East Greenwich', the same tenure under which the Castle Farm was held in 1575. William Lambert's own house is the 'messuage late Fowlers', held of the bailiff and burgesses of the Borough of Buckingham as lords of the manor of Buckingham. This is the same tenure as when 'Fowlers Farm' was conveyed to Francis Dayrell, and then to John Lambert in 1591.

William Lambert was succeeded by his son, John (baptised 28 November 1612). John was then a minor, but he too died in 1632 – before he attained his majority. The next heir was John's sister, Mary. Mary had been baptised on 8 February 1619, and in 1632 was described as 'of the age 13 years, six months and six days'.

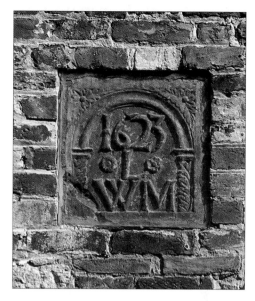

16   Datestone WLM 1623, Castle House.

According to an inquisition post mortem taken at this time, the Lamberts' property in Buckingham consisted of:

> A messuage called the Castle House, and lands in Buckingham and Gawcott, the Manor of Stockholt Barns and 370 acres of land lying in Stockholt, Akeley and Lillingstone Dayrell, holden of New College, and a wood called Three Slades, and 170 acres in Maids Moreton. There were twelve acres of pasture land attached to Castle House, an Orchard near Podd's Lane [Moreton Road], two water mills and a dove house, and various tenements in Buckingham and Gawcott.[10]

Again, the Latin document loses something in the translation; the reference here to 'Castle House' is to the site of the Castle, while the Lamberts' own house, formerly 'Fowlers Farm', seems to be covered by the term 'lands in Buckingham and Gawcott'. The water mills mentioned in the inquisition are in fact the Town Mills. This property must have been purchased by William Lambert in 1613, for the 'Parsonage Mills' or 'Prebend Mills', in the occupation of John Chernell, were specifically excluded from a conveyance of the manor of the Prebend End of Buckingham from Sir Robert Brett to Sir Thomas Denton of Hillesden in that year.[11] The mills passed to William Lambert's daughter, Mary, whose husband Edward Bagot, sold them to Edmund Dayrell in 1659.[12] The manor of Stockholt Barnes was a sub-manor of Akeley which had once belonged to Richard Fowler, but which John Lambert purchased in 1597. It too passed to William Lambert's daughter, Mary Bagot, whose son Walter Bagot sold it to Simon Bennett of Beachampton in 1673.[13]

Sir Edward Richardson

William Lambert's widow subsequently married Sir Edward Richardson, who had been knighted at Welbeck, the seat of Sir William Cavendish, on 10 August 1619. Richardson came to live at Castle House and must have become one of the principal citizens of Buckingham. He acquired further land in the town and was evidently farming on a large scale. In his will of 1637 he leaves most of his property in trust for his wife with remainder to his cousin Thomas Lambert:

> Whereas I did covenant with Francis Crawley Sergeant at Law and now knight and one of His Majesty's Justices of his Court of Common Pleas to leave unto Mary my now wife the sum of one thousand marks at the time of my death. In full discharge of the same I give unto her all my goods and chattels as followeth namely all my horses beasts sheep corn and hay either going or growing upon my grounds or in my barns either in Buckingham or Moreton or elsewhere and also my plate and household stuff whatever.
>
> I further give to her and her heirs for ever the land which I purchased of my sister Lambard lying in the fields of Moreton.
>
> I also give to her and her heirs the tithes of the Grayes Field meadow and closes she and they paying towards the chief rent due to the King the sum of six shillings a year.
>
> I also give her during her life the ten acres of land lying in the fields of Buckingham and the tithes of the Borough of Buckingham she paying towards the King's rent the sum of fifty shillings yearly.
>
> Provided that she my wife shall think that this is not a full satisfaction for her thousand marks then my executors are to pay her the sum according to my covenant and also I give her fifty pounds to buy her a gown.
>
> And after her decease I give the same land and tithes to my cousin Thomas Lambard during his life and after his death to Thomas Lambard my godson and his heirs for ever paying the same rent.
>
> I release to my cousin Thomas Lambard all such money as he oweth me by his statute and I give him more five hundred pounds to be paid unto him one year after my decease.
>
> I give to my daughter Crawley twenty pounds.

Edward Richardson's 'daughter Crawley' is in fact Mary, daughter and heiress of William and Mary Lambert, who was born in 1619. She was married at a very young age to her first cousin, John Crawley of Someries, Bedfordshire. John Crawley had followed his father into the law and, even though still a young man, was already Attorney General to Queen Henrietta Maria. His promising career was cut short by his death early in 1641; the marriage had produced no children. After an unusually short widowhood, Mary married again – at Buckingham on 9 May 1641. Her second husband was Edward Bagot (born at Trescote on 23 May 1616), son and heir of Sir Harvey Bagot of Blithfield, Staffordshire. The Bagots lived principally at Blithfield, but some of their 17 children, 12 sons and five daughters, were baptised at Buckingham. Their mother-in-law, Lady Mary Richardson, with whom they must have stayed on their visits to Castle House, eventually came to live with them at Blithfield and died there in 1659.

The Civil War

It was the Civil War that brought really important visitors to Castle House. Prince Rupert was in Buckingham at the end of June 1643, successfully foiling an attempt to capture him launched from Parliamentary Aylesbury. Royalist soldiers led by Sir Charles Lucas emerged victorious in the encounter at Bint Hill. But, instead of giving battle to the main Parliamentary army commanded by the Earl of Essex, Rupert withdrew to Banbury. At least according to Essex, Rupert's departure caused some surprise, because 'they [the Royalists] had perswaded the people that they would not quit that place untill they had beaten me out of the Countrie'.[11] Essex himself was no stranger to the Buckingham area, having leased the Tithe House in Brackley in the 1630s. But Essex decided not to move into Buckingham itself, although he did send a force commanded by Colonel Middleton 'to clear that Town and Coast, which they did'.[12] While these military manoeuvres were taking place, work was proceeding with the fortification of Hillesden House for the King. We do not know where Prince Rupert stayed during his time in Buckingham. It could have been at Castle House; at the very least he would have called on Lady Richardson. There can be no doubt that virtually everyone connected with Castle House was for the King. Lady Richardson's brother, Sir Francis Crawley, was a prominent Royalist judge who had now joined the King in Oxford. The Bagot family supported the Royal cause in Staffordshire and the many surviving members of the Lambert family in Buckingham were also Royalists. This becomes clear when we examine the story of the most important event of the Civil War in the immediate vicinity of Buckingham, the attack on Hillesden House. The Royalist commander at Hillesden was Colonel Smith, himself a Buckingham man. In January 1644 a Parliamentary force under Captain Jeremiah Abercrombie attacked a small Royalist contingent at Winslow; the royalists fled 'to their Deen which was Sr alexander dentons hous'. Abercrombie followed and then, in his own extraordinary spelling:

> I whild about and tuke bukingham in my way brought five of the townsmen with me whereof on [Richard Potter] was the balli of the town and on other who was father to on of the runaway captaines on Lambert and the three keept them presoners until they payd some arrears due to the steat, likwayes tuke on caviller who had served in your Excellencies [Essex's] army befor I have sent him to salsbari that night I tuke them I carried them to my quarters hard by the enemies quarters to see if Captuine lambart wold come to viset his father but in did he proved a very ondutiful child and veri ongratefal to me who was his friend in proveding a loaging for his father. I think if his fathers and his nebuds fiftie pounds had not proveld mor than his sonnes visitations or if it had tarried as long as his sonne I think hee had gon to Salsbary or london be this tym but it came and they war all release the next day and I desired him to tel his sone that I would tarri on night more on them and if they did not show themselves cavaliers I wold take that nam from them and titule them with the name of Culands and proclaime it openly and make beals to the same effect and put them upon their garrison hous and every poost betwixt my quarters and them if it shold cost me my life.[13]

In other words, it looks as if Abercrombie extorted money from Captain Lambert's relations under threat of sending him as a prisoner to London or Salisbury. In fact, the Royalists slipped away from Hillesden, which was then occupied by Abercrombie for a while. But he was captured in a skirmish at Westbury and the Royalists returned.

When Hillesden finally fell to the Parliamentary forces, on 4 March 1644, 'Captain Lambert' was among the list of prisoners. It is difficult to know which branch of the family Captain Lambert belonged to. He could have been Mr John Lambert, whose burial is recorded on 16 November 1649, or William Lambert, Gentleman, who was buried on 29 August 1665.

Charles I at Castle House

The war was drawing ever closer to Castle House itself and, in a sense, it actually arrived in June 1644. Thus we read in Osborne's Tracts:

> On Saturday, June 22, 1644, the King came to Buckingham to Sir Thomas Richardson's [*actually should be to Sir Edward's or rather to Lady Mary Richardson's*], from Sir Thomas Coghill's House, at Blechington; went Wednesday, June 26, to Brackley, to the College there, and stayed only one Day; went thence to Dedington, to the Parsonage, and thence to Moreton Henmarsh [*Moreton in the Marsh*].

Although earlier owners, notably the Fowlers, had certainly entertained royalty, we cannot be totally sure that Henry VII or Catherine of Aragon stayed at Castle House – though it is highly likely that they did. But with Charles I there can be no doubt. This was surely the moment of Castle House's greatest importance, its finest hour. The King's visit is admirably described in Douglas Elliott's *Buckingham: the Loyal and Ancient Borough* and, above all, in Henry Roundell's wonderful lecture 'Buckingham Town, Buckingham People and their Neighbours during the Civil Wars', delivered to the Buckingham Literary and Scientific Institution on 10 March 1864.

The first sign that something extraordinary was about to happen appeared early in the morning of 22 June. The townspeople awoke to find that the advance guard of a large royal army was entering Buckingham over the Tingewick Bridge. The advance guard was led by the Earl of Cleveland, who swept through Buckingham without stopping to protect the town from any attack from the south or east. But news spread that the King himself was following with the main army and would be staying in Buckingham for a while. Roundell's imaginative reconstruction of the scene remains unsurpassed:

> The Royal entry into Buckingham must have been a goodly sight – The King is arriving now. Let us walk down and see him. It is hard pushing to get down West Street, through the crowd and through the soldiers. But we have struggled on, past Mr Richard Potter's house on the right hand side; we have gained the little public house at the corner – now the Barrel – then the King's Arms, a low thatched picturesque building, most of us remember it; and we have gained too the window of an upstairs room and can look down on the gallant show beneath. All the space is filled with soldiers, line after line, as far as the eye can reach along the Brackley Road. Castle House – the present residence of Mr Hearn – is hastily prepared to receive the Royal Visitor. High above its roof floats the King's Standard. Carpets and rugs have been brought out to cover the path-way. On either side from the gateway to the door stand the flower of England's nobility and gentry. At the gate, the Lady Richardson, mistress of the house, ready to pay homage to her Sovereign – Charles, himself the most graceful horseman in his army, rides through the ranks of the serried troopers, his gold-plated armour gleaming in the sunshine, his tall plumes nodding in the summer air, and with a stately courtesy to his hostess, passes on and treads perchance on the selfsame step over which many of us have passed to enjoy the hospitality of its present owner.
>
> The crowd disperses. The soldiers betake themselves to their Quarters. One musketeer with loaded firelock paces up and down before the Castle House. Another marches backwards and forwards along the terraced slope within the

garden. Further back a cordon of guards is drawn round the house. Beyond them the sentries; on the Castle Hill, on the Pightle, at the Butcher Row, at the Drapery. Death to any man approaching within ear-shot of the Chamber where the King and his Generals hold high Council of War.[14]

The town, which had certainly displayed more sympathy for the Royal cause than for that of Parliament, had a wonderful opportunity to prove its loyalty and devotion. Of course, the most obvious way of gauging a town's loyalty was the comfort of the quarters and the quantity and quality of the provisions it made available. The Bailiff, Thomas Napton, faced a formidable task; he had to find quarters for some 12,000 men and stabling for 3,000 horses. Buckingham had not seen anything like it since Catherine of Aragon's even bigger army in 1513. Fortunately for Napton, the Parliamentary forces in the area had not expected the arrival of the King's army. Elliot notes that this meant that 'many carts containing wine, groceries and tobacco, travelling along what they thought were secure roads, were captured by the royalist troops and brought in triumph to Buckingham'. The captured provisions would have helped to relieve the burden of victualling and supplying the King's soldiers.

While many Royalist soldiers probably had to sleep under the stars, there was no question about the King's quarters. If Charles had come to Buckingham a few months earlier, he would have had a choice and might have decided to stay in the, probably slightly larger, Prebendal House. We do not know exactly what happened to the Prebendal House, which appears so prominently in Speed's map of 1610. It is likely, however, that the Manor House, owned by Sir Alexander Denton, was destroyed at the time of the attack on his other house at Hillesden. With both of his houses destroyed and Denton a broken man in Parliamentary custody in London, there was no alternative to Lady Richardson and Castle House. In any case, there is no suggestion that the Prebendal House had undergone anything like the thorough 'makeover' that William Lambert had undertaken at Castle House. Even if the Prebendal House had still been standing, Charles would probably have gone to Castle House. Furthermore there is every sign that the owners of the house, Lady Richardson and her family, were strong supporters of the Royalist cause.

During Saturday 22 June the King held a Council of War in the great parlour at Castle House, created by the Lamberts some twenty-five years earlier. The King sat on the elevated dais at the upper end of the parlour. Below him and on either side sat the Councillors in order of rank. On Charles's right sat Sir Edward Walker (Secretary at War), then the Earl of Bainforth and Forth (Lord Lieutenant-General of the Army), the Earl of Lindsay (Lord High Chamberlain), and finally Lord Wilmot (Master of the Horse). To the King's left sat the Duke of Richmond, Lord Digby (Secretary of State), Sir John Colepepper (Master of the Rolls) and Sir Jacob Asteley (Sergeant Major-General of the Army). Over the centuries, there have been many gatherings of important people at Castle House, but none can rival the group that assembled on 22 June 1644. No doubt the King, a lover of fine architecture and paintings, admired William Lambert's splendid room, but there were urgent matters to discuss. Although the King could still muster impressive forces, by the summer of 1644 his chances of ultimate victory were beginning to fade. In the early days of the war, the Parliamentary commanders and armies had not been notably better than those fighting for the King – if indeed they were as good. Now, however, with the creation of the New Model Army and the emergence of commanders like Cromwell and Fairfax, the King's enemies enjoyed a clear superiority. As the war went on, the fact that Parliament controlled the richer parts of the country – especially London – became ever more telling. To avoid defeat, Charles would have to come up with something really remarkable. The Council opened with a few formal orders – for sending carts and teams to Oxford, and for the supply of arms and provisions. But then came the serious business – the plan of campaign. Some Members of the Council proposed an advance on the 'Associated Counties' of Northampton, Bedford and Cambridge; in other words, they proposed an attack on the heartland of Parliamentary territory. Others wanted to march northwards to join with Prince Rupert, and then the united Royal armies would deal with Sir William Waller in Worcestershire and with Essex in Dorset. The debate went on, with the King seeming to favour one view and then the other. Characteristically, Charles was against any hasty decision: 'The matter is of mighty importance. It cannot be determined lightly.' So far there was one Councillor who had not spoken at all, Lord Wilmot, and the King now asked for his opinion. When Wilmot began to speak it became obvious that he had a radically different plan:

> If it please your Majesty, neither of these plans is good. I abhor these timid counsels – Waller is behind us three days march. Essex is in Dorsetshire. We have eight thousand men – let us march upon London. Newport Pagnell has but three hundred in its Garrison. Aylesbury less than six hundred. We will trample them under foot. From St Albans we will send a message to Parliament and the City. We shall learn what is the true affection of the City of London to your Majesty, of which they speak so much. My voice is 'Towards London'. If it please your Majesty we march by day break tomorrow and every Soldier will shout 'Long live the King'.

According to Lord Clarendon, no-one, not even the King, had had any prior inkling of what Wilmot now proposed. To begin with his scheme was received in stunned silence, but then a lively debate followed. The King appeared restless and uneasy and did not know how to respond. Typically, he decided to seek a compromise and to place responsibility on others:

> Wilmot's advice is in part good. Let an address to the City and the Parliament be drawn up, that We decree. For the other matter, it is of the gravest consideration. Let Lord Digby and the Master of the Rolls return to Oxford forthwith, and lay this plan before the Lords of the Council, and if they approve we will march towards London. Meanwhile, it is Our Order that the army remain in its quarters. The Council is dissolved.

Clarendon did not think highly of Wilmot or his plan, describing it as 'this extravagant notion'. Clarendon had doubts about Wilmot's loyalty; there were rumours that he wanted to make a deal with the Earl of Essex and then the two commanders would impose a solution on King and Parliament alike. Clarendon says that, during his stay in Buckingham, Charles I was troubled by 'ill humour and faction' in his own army and believes that Wilmot was to blame. The Master of the Horse appeared 'sullen and perverse, and every day grew more insolent'. In particular, Wilmot engaged in constant intrigues against other members of the Kings Council, especially Digby and Colepepper. While in Buckingham, Wilmot actually drew up a petition, which he encouraged his officers to sign, begging the King to remove his rivals from the

Council. In large measure, Roundell appears to follow Clarendon, describing Wilmot as 'the promoter of faction in Charles's army, the man who loved his King partly and himself wholly'. According to Clarendon, Wilmot's plan 'troubled the King very much' and he implies that Charles would have preferred to squash the proposal there and then. But the King 'thought it not fit absolutely to reject it' because he feared that this would only encourage Wilmot to press ahead with the petition against Digby and Colepepper. Yet the fact that Charles insisted that Digby and Colepepper – Wilmot's enemies – should present the plan to the Council in Oxford, strongly suggests that he was not looking for a favourable response.

The King was happy to wait. On the Sunday, Buckingham church was filled to overflowing with the King's soldiers. Monday 24 June was devoted to celebrations and festivities. A courier brought news that, on 16 June, the Queen had given birth to a healthy daughter at Exeter. The child was to be christened Henrietta after her mother. The King was delighted and his joy was increased when his eldest son, the future Charles II, arrived in Buckingham in time to join the celebrations. After the acrimonious Council meeting, perhaps it would be unfair to criticise the King for taking a day or so to relax.

On Tuesday, Digby and Colepepper returned from Oxford, but 'without any approbation of the march or the message by the lords'. There was one further development before Wilmot's scheme was finally abandoned: 'but all that intrigue fell of itself upon the sure intelligence that Waller had left Worcestershire and marched out with what speed he could to find his Majesty'.[15] In other words, with Waller hard on his heels, the King could not possibly contemplate marching towards London. He had no alternative but to move westwards to meet Waller, fighting the inconclusive Battle of Cropredy Bridge. The King then moved to Evesham.

Despite doubts about Wilmot, Roundell also criticises the King. Valuable time was being lost. 'Three days passed – days of which every hour was of priceless value.' It might have been better if Charles had adopted any of the three plans discussed at Castle House. If he had gone north, 'Marston Moor might have remained to this day a bloodless field'. If he had attacked the Associated Counties, 'he would have cut off at their sources the chief springs whence the Parliament drew its supplies of men and money for its exhausted armies'. Above all, if he had marched towards London, 'no force could have been collected to bar his progress, and it is not impossible, he might have dictated his own terms of peace, to a reluctant but defenceless Parliament'.

In the end, Roundell hints that Charles should have ignored any personal hostility towards Wilmot and endorsed his plan, not least because news of the King's presence in Buckingham and the possibility of an advance on London had caused panic in the capital. Leonard Sharpe, a Parliamentary spy in the King's army, supplied his masters with detailed information about the debate at Buckingham. Is it possible that Sharpe managed to evade the guards and slip into Castle House? Parliamentary Journals, usually anxious to put a favourable interpretation on the military situation, were quite open in their expressions of alarm. The *Parliament Scout* admitted frankly, 'Sunday and Monday, we were almost overcome with feares of the King's powers'. Roundell's ultimate verdict on the King is damning:

> Charles, by that indecision of movement and want of plan which made Edge
> Hill and every battle he won a fruitless victory, by which he finally permitted

his enemies to collect and crush him at Naseby, lost the golden opportunity which fortune offered him, and on the very day he left Buckingham had so little fixedness of purpose, that he changed the direction of his march from Bletchington near Oxford, to quarter his troops at Brackley.

While it is true that Charles was a notoriously indecisive man, he seems to have been even more hesitant than usual during his visit to Buckingham. It has to be acknowledged that Wilmot's plan was extremely risky but is it possible that there was another reason for Charles' indecision? Another of the King's characteristics was that he was very superstitious. According to legend, during his time in Buckingham, Charles asked a courtier to find out if there was anything in the history of the town that could provide an 'omen' for his cause. After making a few enquiries, the delighted courtier returned to tell the King that Buckingham was a place of good, even wonderful omen. Just as a courier had now brought the good news of the birth of a healthy daughter to the King, so, many years earlier, another courier had also brought good news to a Queen – this time of a great English victory. The Queen concerned had actually been staying in the very house where Charles himself was now lodged. In short, it would be hard to think of an omen more favourable.

But it is important to remember that Charles himself had stayed in Scotland for some years after his father inherited the English throne, not moving south until after the death of his elder brother, Prince Henry. In many ways, Charles was really more Scottish than English and he spoke with a marked Scots accent. Thus he asked the courtier 'Aye, and victory over whom?' The now thoroughly embarrassed courtier, was forced to admit that the great English victory – Flodden Field – had been over the Scots. Catherine of Aragon, no blood relation of Charles, may have rejoiced, but the King would have remembered that in 1513 the English had killed his own great-great grandfather, King James IV of Scotland. For the superstitious Charles, Castle House was thus a place of very bad omen indeed. Perhaps he even wondered if the 'omen' meant that the 't'English' would eventually kill him as they had killed his direct ancestor, James IV. 'T'English' were to do exactly that in January 1649.

Of course, for such a superstitious man, the fact that Buckingham appeared a town of such ill omen would have made it the last place from which to launch such a hazardous undertaking. But, whatever the reason for Charles' caution, his position was now so desperate that it might have been wiser for him to agree to Wilmot's bold plan. It could just have succeeded. We must ask, therefore, whether Castle House was the place where the King really lost the Civil War? If so, Catherine of Aragon and her Fowler hosts were still influencing events more than one hundred years after their deaths. We might even see Charles' mistake as 'Catherine's revenge' on the monarchies of both England and Scotland.

The Bagot Family

The Bagot family were much involved in the Civil War. Sir Harvey Bagot's fourth son, Richard, commanded the royal garrison based in the Cathedral Close at Lichfield and raised a regiment of horse for the King. Another son, Harvey, raised a regiment of foot and Sir Harvey himself moved into Lichfield from Blithfield to stay with the garrison. Richard Bagot died of wounds received at the Battle of Naseby and was buried in Lichfield Cathedral. But Edward Bagot does not seem to have taken up arms; he and Mary spent most of their time at Blithfield, although it is clear that they visited Buckingham regularly. Edward Bagot's inactivity, compared to the military prowess of his brothers, attracts a slightly barbed comment in *Memorials of the Bagot Family*:

> Sir Edward Bagot appears to have dwelt under his vine and his fig tree at Blithfield, whilst his younger brothers, Hervey and Richard, were using their swords on the part of Charles I.

Edward and Mary's third child, Edward, born at Blithfield on 18 March 1643, died at Buckingham in 1646. The ninth child, Mary, was born at Buckingham in May 1650 and died shortly afterwards. The twelfth, William, was born at Buckingham on 26 February 1653.

It is clear that the Bagots were deeply affected by the death of their eldest son, Harvey, born on St Valentine's Day 1642, on 22 October 1655. Lady Bagot commissioned the poet John Middleton to write some moving obituary verses:

> O Dearest Hall, whom nature thus endued
> To shew, if she were old her youth's renewed.
> A noble branch of a twice noble tree –
> Grand hopes and ornament of his Familie.
> Devoted to all virtues, acute sage,
> Nothing not manly in him but his Age!
> But thirteene springs seene yet so above toyes
> That in comparison, most long beards are boys.
> To whom obedience, love and pyety
> Were naturall as 'tis for birds to fly.
> Att Buckingham hee's ill, at Stamford lyes
> Weake and infirme Thence moved to Blithfield dyes.[16]

Mary Bagot seems to have remained on good terms with her first husband's family and Judge Crawley was one of Harvey Bagot's godparents. Lady Richardson was another and she was also godmother to Anne (born 14 March 1643). As late as 1658, Lady Richardson was godmother to the twins, Harvey and Edward, born 12 May. Lady Richardson made her home with her daughter and son-in-law. As she had married William Lambert in the early years of the century, she must have been quite old by the late 1650s. She died on 27 August 1658 and was buried at Blithfield. After summarising the story of her life, her Latin memorial describes her as 'Haec Matrona insignis', or 'This remarkable woman'.

Although the Bagots were now based in Staffordshire, they still retained some links with Buckingham. The Bagots' ninth child, the appropriately named Lambert (born 2 August 1649), lived for a time at Maids Moreton. In the 1640s and '50s Edward and Mary Bagot continued to grant leases on town properties and on farmland in a way not very different to the pattern of the days of the Bartons and Fowlers. On 20 April 1659 Sir Edward Bagot and Dame Mary his wife granted an 11-year lease of Conduit Field, the meadow adjoining, Grayes Field and Cheynells Close to Pelham Sandwell of Buckingham gentleman at a rent of £34 per year. On 30 September 1662, Sir Edward Bagot and Dame Mary his wife gave a 99-year lease of a piece of ground on Castle Hill 'whereon a barn and stable stand' to George Robins of Buckingham gentleman for a rent of 2s. per year. But the fact that some of the leases were for 99 years suggests that the Bagots' interest in Buckingham

17   Sir Edward Bagot, *c*.1660.   **18**   Lady Mary Bagot, *c*. 1660.

was declining. Amongst the properties Edward and Mary Bagot had inherited from the Lamberts was the Town Mill, now part of the University of Buckingham. The earliest document in the University's deed parcel is a fine following the 1659 sale of the mill to Edmund Dayrell gentleman. The Dayrells had not been quite beaten.

The 1667 Sale of Castle House

The Bagots finally disposed of their Buckingham property on 15 September 1667. The conveyance was between Sir Edward Bagot 'of Blythfield Staffs Knight & Baronett and Dame Mary his wife' and Stephen Monteage, 'of London gent and Jane his wife'. By that time, Castle House was once more occupied by tenants. The deed of sale refers to:

> All that Capital Messuage or Mansion house now or late in the possession or occupation of Richard Burton gent or his assigns Together with all wainscotte hereditaments and appurtenances thereunto belonging or therewith now used situate within the town or parish of Buckingham within the County.

The sale included the site of Buckingham Castle and the following farmland:

> Two closes lying behind the said Messuage (20a)
> One Meadow Close by or near the said Messuage (10a)
> Grayes Field and Cheynells Close (24a)
> Conduit Field with 2a of Meadow thereunto adjoining Castle Hill Field

The property remained charged with:

One fee farm rent of £6 1s. 4d. parcell of a greater fee farm charged upon one William Lambart deceased for a messuage and 6 acres of land, parcel of a late Chantry called Barton's Chantry in the town of Buckingham.

The sale price was £1,765.[10] About the same time, the Bagots also sold another Lambert property, the Manor of Stockholt in the Parish of Akeley.[11] Sir Edward Bagot died on 30 March 1673, aged 56. A monument to his memory in Blithfield church describes him as 'a true assertor of Episcopacy in the Church and Hereditary Monarchy in the State'. After the Restoration, Bagot became a Member of Parliament for Staffordshire and 'by his affable Temper, constant Hospitality, and inviolable integrity in doing Justice, he drew to himself the love and esteem of all'.

The Will of Mary Bagot, 1686

In her last years, Lady Mary Bagot made her home with her daughter Mary and her son-in-law Sir William Newdigate. She died at the Newdigate's house at Arbury, Warwickshire, on 22 October 1686, but was subsequently buried at Blithfield. Although the link with Buckingham was now broken, Lady Bagot remembered the town in her will:

> I give and bequeath unto ye Corporacon of the Towne of Buckingham in the Countie of Buckingham ye sume of one hundred pounds to be paid unto them within the space of one yeare next after my decease upon Speciall Trust and confidence and to the intent and purpose that that they shall therewith (with what convenient speede they can) purchase Lands to them selves and Successors in Fee Simple and with the Rents issues and profitts thereof yearlie and every yeare for ever at or about the Feast of the Nativity of our Lord and Saviour Jesus Christ provide and bestowe Five Gownes with the Letters: M.B. - sett in Black Cloth upon the Breasts of the same upon Five of the poorest widowes from tyme to tyme comorant & dwelling within the said Town. And my minde & will is that the yearely proffitt or interest that shall and may with safety be raised of and by the said one hundred pounds from and after the time it shall be paid untill Lands shall be purchased with it as afroesaid shall be bestowed and imployed to & in the uses before mentioned in manner and forme as is before expressed.

Browne Willis had a high opinion of the Bagot family and, when writing in the 1730s, still hoped that they would continue to be generous to Buckingham. He pointed out the Bagots were linked to Buckingham in two ways, distantly related to the Stafford Dukes of Buckingham and, also, through Mary Bagot. He trusted that the present representatives of the Bagot, Chester and Newdigate families, Mary's great grandchildren, would 'never be found wanting in shewing their utmost regard to it' [Buckingham].

Stephen Monteage

By the time of Lady Bagot's death, Castle House had changed hands once more. The Monteage family owned it for a brief 13 years. It is striking that Browne Willis, who has so much to say about the Bagots, virtually ignores the Monteages. He approves of the Bagots, with their steadfast support for Charles I and their ancient lineage; their motto, Antiquam Obtens (Possessing Antiquity), represents everything he believed in. The origins of the Monteages were more obscure and the fact that there are two Stephen Monteages makes their story difficult to unravel. The purchaser of Castle House was Stephen Monteage sen., a London merchant with no known earlier links with Buckingham. Monteage's children had been born in the 1620s, so he must have been quite elderly by 1667. Jane Monteage, probably Stephen's second wife, and her mother, Anne, widow of Edward Deane of Pinnock, Gloucestershire, certainly lived at Castle House. After the Great Plague of London in 1665, followed by the Fire in 1666, wealthy merchants became especially eager to acquire a safe place of residence in the country for their families. Sadly, Buckingham was not particularly healthy in the 1660s – there were several epidemics of smallpox – and Mrs Deane died on 26 December 1669 and her daughter, Mrs Monteage, in 1670. A joint memorial in the old Buckingham church described them as 'singular Examples of Piety and Virtue'. Despite his advanced years, Stephen Monteage decided to return to London.

Yet there may be more links between the Monteages and Buckingham than has been appreciated. Although we know little about Stephen Monteage sen., there is considerably more information about his son, Stephen Monteage jun., born 1623, who merits an entry in the *Dictionary of National Biography*. By 1667 Stephen Monteage jun., already in his forties, was a successful merchant in his own right. He had been apprenticed to John Houblon, a merchant trading to Spain and a prominent member of the Grocers Company. Monteage remained a close friend of the Houblon family throughout his life. Another member of the Grocers Company was John Fleet, also a friend of the Houblons. Readers will recognise Fleet as one of the worst villains in Browne Willis's version of the history of Buckingham. In the chapter *Famous Men born in the Parish*, Browne Willis vilifies Fleet, 'who was Lord Mayor of London, Anno 1693, born at Boreton and apprenticed thence by Charity, yet a man so destitute of gratitude, as not to contribute the least Charity to his native Parish, in any of its greatest Exigencies'. Given the links between Stephen Monteage jun., Houblon and Fleet, could it be that Fleet suggested Buckingham as a suitable place of retirement for Monteage's parents and grandmother?

While Browne Willis attacks Fleet for his meanness in failing to repay the debt of gratitude to Buckingham, there was another reason for his dislike. Browne Willis was a high Tory and Fleet and Houblon were early Whigs, the leaders of the party in the City of London. Their careers really took off after the Revolution of 1688. Houblon became the first Governor of the Bank of England and Fleet, Governor of the East India Company. Monteage himself died in 1687,[17] but his political outlook was probably much the same as that of his friends. In other words, the change of ownership in 1667 marked a distinct change in the political 'colour' of Castle House. Once so traditionalist and royalist, it now entered a Whig period.

But Stephen Monteage was important for other reasons. The *DNB* describes him as a 'merchant and accountant', a man who 'did much towards bringing into general use the method of keeping accounts by double entry'. He published two books: *Debtor and Creditor* (1675) and *Instructions for Rent-gatherers: Accompts &c made easie* (1683). Thus Monteage can be regarded as one of the founders of modern accounting. His financial expertise raises another interesting question: why did the Bagots sell, especially to people they probably regarded with some distaste? It should be remembered that loyalty to the King in the Civil War had been costly. A few Royalists had their estates confiscated, but many more, including the Bagots, were subjected to heavy fines. On 29 April 1647 Sir Harvey Bagot 'Compounded his Deliquency', that is he was assessed to pay a fine of £1,340 for his royalism. At a time when Bagot's annual income was around £500 per annum, this must have been a heavy burden. In 1648 Sir Harvey Bagot was described as 'much in debt'. In 1656 the old Royalist was reduced to petitioning Oliver Cromwell to waive the fine. Bagot went to the lengths of addressing Cromwell as 'Your Highness' and stressed his 'active and passive obedience' to the present government. It is unlikely that he had any real respect for Cromwell and he must have felt humiliated putting his name to a rather grovelling petition. But it did no good and the fine was not lifted.

Although welcomed for other reasons, the Restoration of Charles II brought no financial respite. In 1660 confiscated estates were returned to their rightful owners, but no compensation was given to those who had been fined for their royalism. Many raised the necessary sums by borrowing. Stephen Monteage and his associates were just the sort of men to have been interested in this sort of business. Of course, the Bagots had a huge family to provide for and the reference to 'constant hospitality' in Edward Bagot's memorial suggests a man who was free with his money. Could it be that Bagot was already in debt to the Monteages and was forced to transfer the property when he found it hard to maintain the payments on a loan from them? The fact that the Bagots' son, Walter (born 1649), later married an heiress – Jane, daughter of Charles Salisbury of Bachymbydd, Denbighshire – suggests that the family fortunes were in need of repair. Even if the Bagots were not too straitened, they may have had plans for the improvement of Blithfield, and the realisation of assets and/or the reduction of debt would have made good sense.

The shift of ownership from the country gentry and Royalist Bagots to the London-oriented, mercantile and Whig-inclined Monteages marks another change in the role and perception of Castle House. No doubt it was still regarded with affection, but there are hints of a more hard-headed outlook. Castle House was a piece of property, a financial asset. In the last resort, it was something to be used and made to work as part of the grand strategy of wealth-making and fortune-building.

As we have seen, it is possible that the Bagots mortgaged Castle House to pay their fines for Royalism – but this is only a guess. We can be certain, however, that the Monteages also mortgaged the property. One of the advantages of a place like Castle House was that it provided a good security. Hence, money could be borrowed 'against' it on better terms or at lower rates of interest than would have been possible with an unsecured loan or with one where the value of the security was less certain – for example stock in trade. The attractions of raising money on mortgage for a London merchant faced with the vagaries of commerce are obvious. He could either use his country house to raise money to see him through in times of depression or, if business were good, raise cash quickly to take advantage of a favourable opportunity. There were many ready to advance the necessary funds. In 1678 Stephen Monteage and his son Deane mortgaged their property in Buckingham to Peter Clayton and Anthony Kerk of London, gentlemen.

City merchants often married late and died comparatively young. Their widows, unable or unwilling to engage in active trading themselves, looked for a safe investment and lending on mortgage offered the ideal solution. On 2 April 1680 Stephen Monteage of the Parish of Allhallows on the Wall in the City of London, merchant, mortgaged Castle House to Elizabeth Glover of St Sepulchres, London, widow, for the sum of £500. But the arrangement did not last long; perhaps Monteage decided he needed more cash. On 30 September 1680 he sold Castle House and the remaining land to John Rogers the elder of Buckingham for £1,930. At the time of the 1680 sale, Castle House was once more occupied by a tenant, a widow named Jane Cutler. The purchaser, John Rogers, did not have all of the cash required, but Widow Glover was willing to oblige once more and, on 2 October 1680, provided another loan on mortgage – this time to Rogers – for the larger sum of £922 10s. A new phase in the story of Castle House was about to begin, aided by what we might call 'The Widow Glover Building Society'.

It is always interesting to link the history of a house to what was happening in the nation as a whole. If we look back over the period from the time William Lambert took over in 1611 until the sale to John Rogers in 1680, it is clear that Castle House had had two distinct phases or 'orientations'. The splendid improvements of the Jacobean age culminating in the visit of Charles I point to an orientation, or at least an aspiration, towards the Court – and the Court was still the focus of national life at this time. Then there was the crucial break of the Interregnum. The monarchy came back in 1660 and the court became important once more – but not as important as it had been before. Now commerce and, above all, the City became a rival focus of power and Castle House followed suit. But if the Lamberts and the Bagots turned Castle House towards the court and the Monteages turned it towards the City, what would be Castle House's character in the new phase that was about to dawn?

Chapter Five

THE ROGERS FAMILY:
BREWING AND REBUILDING

IN SOME WAYS, the sale to John Rogers in 1680 allowed Castle House to revert to its traditional role. As in the days of the Lamberts, the house was occupied by its owners rather than by tenants. But there were other similarities with the Lamberts. Whereas the Monteages had been 'in-comers' who never had deep roots in Buckingham, the Rogers were a local family. With them, the Lamberts' story seems to repeat itself; once more, we see a pattern of local traders, rising generation by generation till they reach the pinnacle of Buckingham society represented by Castle House. Indeed, as with the Lamberts, the Rogers' purchase of Castle House could be seen in the context of a wider programme of property acquisitions in the Buckingham area after the Lambert estate had been largely 'dispersed' by the Bagots' sales.

The Rise of the Rogers Family

The surname Rogers occurs widely in Buckinghamshire and elsewhere; clearly not all those who bear it are related and this makes the construction of family trees and pedigrees difficult. There were a number of Rogers families in North Bucks in the late 17th and early 18th centuries – and there may have been links between them. Joseph Rogers founded a school at Winslow in 1723 and gave a paten to St Lawrence's Church in the same year.[1] In the church at Newport Pagnell there is a memorial to a John Rogers who died in 1726. This Rogers had a coat of arms, 'A chevron between three harts'.[2] It is tempting to think that this is none other than John Rogers jun. of Buckingham, who had some property in Newport Pagnell and who died in 1727. If the 'old reckoning' had been used, 1727 might well have been 1726, but, sadly, it seems that the two are not the same.

There had certainly been a Rogers family in Buckingham for several generations. A William Rogers of Bourton, yeoman, made his will in 1610, leaving bequests, mostly of calves or sheep, to numerous relatives including a son, John Rogers, and a grandson, also John Rogers. Browne Willis's list of notable burials in Buckingham includes Mathias Rogers, 1600, John Rogers (probably the son of William Rogers of Bourton), 1648 and a Mr Mathias Rogers in 1651. In 1673 John Rogers, a draper (probably the grandson of William Rogers of Bourton), was chosen as Bailiff of Buckingham. We will call him John Rogers senior.

It was John Rogers senior who purchased Castle House and Castle Hill in 1680, although he now described himself as a merchant, a 'step up' from his former position as draper; John Rogers was obviously rising in the world, but it is not clear where he made his money. Although he clearly maintained close links with the town, he may well have spent time in London, or perhaps East Anglia, and could have made much of his money away from Buckingham. The fact that several of his children married people from other parts of the country suggests that he had wide-ranging contacts. In other words, he may not have been so different from the Monteages after all. If, as seems likely, John Rogers senior was born shortly before 1610, he would have been in his early seventies in 1680. He appears to have married twice, although we do not know the name of his first wife. His eldest son – who we will call John Rogers junior – was born about 1650, a time when the Buckingham parish registers are incomplete, probably owing to the effects of the Civil War. There is a record of John Rogers senior's second marriage, to Anne Worfield, at Buckingham on 30 October 1656. The baptisms of several of their daughters appear in the Buckingham parish registers: Katherine in 1657, Martha in 1659 and Anne in 1666. Martha and Anne – though perhaps not Katherine – were unmarried at the time of their father's death. There were also three sons, Edward, James and William. Although their dates of birth are not known, all are described as under the age of 22 and unmarried at the time of their father's death in 1681. These sons are clearly children of John Rogers senior's second marriage.

When John Rogers senior came to make his will, the 'draper' of 1673, and the 'merchant' at the time of the purchase of Castle House, had become a 'gentleman'. The change is significant and it was probably the possession of Castle House that made all the difference. As we have seen, earlier owners of Castle House had had a good deal of land in Buckingham and elsewhere. But the Bagots had largely dispersed the Lamberts' estate and now Castle House and Castle Hill together did not really constitute an estate big enough to be appropriate for a 'landed gentleman'. Yet Castle House was still appropriate for a 'gentleman' and his family, especially if he had important assets elsewhere. There were an increasing number of 'gentlemen' who were not 'landed' in the true sense of the word. They might own some land, but their main income came from business or the professions. Such occupations were not incompatible with the status of gentleman. But acceptance was not automatic and much depended upon where the merchant or lawyer lived and upon how he behaved. Possession of Castle House, with all its historic associations, went a long way to conferring the status of gentleman on its owner. But did John Rogers senior, or at least his heirs, aspire to go higher and move up to become 'landed gentlemen' themselves?

At first sight, the date of John Rogers senior's will – 23 March 1680 – poses a problem. As we have seen, Stephen Monteage sold Castle House to Rogers on 30 September 1680, with Widow Glover providing a mortgage on 2 October, yet in Rogers' will, apparently made several months earlier, Castle House already appears to be his. However, the problem is easily resolved, because in the 1680s the year was reckoned to run from Lady Day to Lady Day. Thus, in modern terms, the date of the will was 23 March 1681 rather than 23 March 1680.

A Family Strategy?

Despite his relatively advanced age, John Rogers senior's will shows signs of having been made in haste; perhaps he was taken ill unexpectedly. It seems that he had already made a bargain to convey Castle House, here described as 'the Mansion House with the appurtenances also the little houses near unto thereunto adjoining and belonging and two closes of pasture ground' to his son John [Rogers junior].

But the formalities had not yet been completed – 'though the writings are not made'. The rest of the property recently purchased from Stephen Monteage is left to Anne, 'my well beloved wife ... during the term of her natural life'. Anne is, however, required to release 'that part of my now dwelling house now in my possession' to their son Edward when he reaches the age of twenty-two. After Anne's death, the property should pass to Edward, James, William, Katherine, Martha and Anne and be divided equally between them. There are also legacies of £400 to Edward, £600 each to James and William, and £600 each to Martha and Anne. Apart from her eventual share in the estate on her mother's death, there is no specific legacy left to Katherine; presumably she was already married and provided with a suitable dowry.

At first sight, the provision for John Rogers junior – apparently the only surviving child from the first marriage – seems ungenerous compared to that received by his half-brothers and sisters. John Rogers senior merely forgives a debt of £200 owed to him by John junior and that 'upon condition that he shall assist my wife in the management of her affairs and trade'. Clearly Anne Rogers was expected to carry on her husband's business. She must have been considerably younger than him and survived until 1708, when she died, probably in London, at the house of her daughter and son-in-law, Katherine and John Sindry.

The will suggests that John Rogers senior was a wealthy man. Just before his death he had laid out £1,930 on the purchase of Castle House, Castle Hill and about 70 acres of land to the west of the town. Even if he had hoped to recoup half that sum by selling Castle House to John Rogers junior, it is remarkable that he was able to leave Castle Hill and legacies totalling £2,800 to his younger children. There was, however, a potential complication in the will – which again points to haste. If John Rogers junior had bought Castle House and the Castle Hill property – which included the Conduit House – went to others, there would have to be agreements to maintain the water system created by the Lamberts.

Although the will seems to give little to John Rogers junior, there is no evidence that father and son were on bad terms. If they had been, it is unlikely that John senior would have asked his son to assist Anne Rogers with her business. John junior may have received his main inheritance before his father's death, probably when he had married a few years earlier. Or John junior could have already been a wealthy man in his own right. Perhaps John junior had followed the probable course of his father's career and had business interests in other parts of the country. The stipulation that he should merely assist his stepmother in the management of her business suggests that he was expected to be away a good deal. The signs are that John Rogers senior and John Rogers junior were business partners. The sale of Castle House from father to son almost immediately after the purchase from Stephen Monteage may have been intended as a 'joint venture' from the start.

The marriages of John Rogers junior's half-sisters were to play an important role in the family's history. Katherine was probably already married in 1681; her husband was John Sindry of St Sepulchres, London, haberdasher. No doubt helped by the substantial legacies from their father, Martha and Ann soon found husbands. Martha married John Gore, a brewer, also of St Sepulchres. Gore must have seemed a particularly good catch. His uncle, Sir George Gore, became a Director of the Bank of England and was to be Lord Mayor of London in 1702. Ann, John Rogers senior's

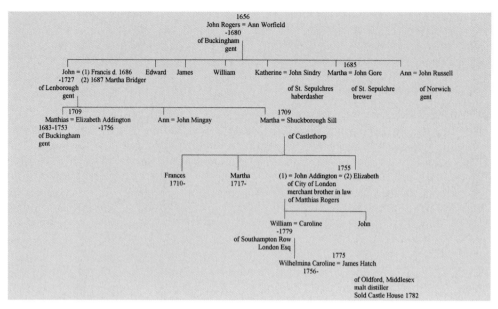

19 Rogers family tree.

youngest daughter, married John Russell of Norwich, gentleman, at Buckingham in 1685.

These marriages raise interesting questions. Sir George Gore, a prominent Whig, moved in the same circles as Stephen Monteage and Sir John Fleet. Even more intriguing is the role of Widow Glover, who provided money on mortgage for both Monteage and Rogers. Mrs Glover had local connections and was a cousin of the (later notorious) Revd. John Mason of Water Stratford. Like John Sindry and John Gore, she now lived in the parish of St Sepulchres, London. Could Mrs Glover have been a matchmaker as well as a source of money on mortgage?

John Rogers junior was now head of the family. If we are right in thinking that he was born around 1650, he would have been about thirty in 1681 and was already married. John and his first wife Frances had at least five children, but several died in infancy. The ultimate heir, Matthias, was baptised in 1683. Frances Rogers died in 1686 and was buried at Buckingham. Although John Rogers was to marry again, he clearly cherished the memory of his first wife. When he came to make his will, almost forty years later, he stipulated: 'My body to the earth whence it came to be decently and in Christian like manner interred therein in the parish church of Buckingham near to the place where my wife Frances lyeth.' By the early 1680s, therefore, the man always referred as 'Mr John Rogers' lived – at least for some of the time – at Castle House. He was probably the most important man in the town and he certainly lived in the most prestigious house. The status of Castle House was such that it was used to accommodate the Judges who came to Buckingham to conduct the Assizes. In 1684 there was an outbreak of smallpox in Buckingham, which might have caused the Assizes to be held in Aylesbury. In order to avoid this calamity, the burgesses wrote to Sir Richard Temple at his house in Covent Garden, urging him to use his influence to ensure that the Assizes were held in Buckingham as usual:

Bucks June ye 5th 84

In order to those greate untruths wee are Sensible are alleadged against our Towne as to ye small Pox being soe very rife amongst us wee shall therefore give you a true Account of ye Condicion of our Towne as itt now stands and hathe Stood for some time past. Since last Alholantide there have beene betweene thirty and Forty families visited but now att this time there is not above Eight families (wherein any one is sick) whereof two are in ye Streete that leads from Paxtons Bridge to Mr Hugh Etherseys and two in ye Streete where ye Judges used to lodge and but one petty Alehouse by the Free Schoole. All the rest of ye Inns and Alehouses in ye Borough and hart of ye Towne Wee doe confidently Assure you are free from the distemper the greatest parte hitherto havinge been in Bourton hold and Churchend. Mr John Rogers his family is cleare but there is a Tennant in one parte of his house whose family hath been visited but are well againe Soe that if the Judge who comes this Circuite bee unwilling to make that his house wee shall provide some other convenient house that shall bee fitt for his recepcon Mrs Playdells and all other private houses who did usually lodge people Att Assize time being free from ye distemper. And if this will not bee satisfactory wee desire you would lett us know in what method to proceed. Humbly desireing (on the behalf of our Selves and of ye Towne) your Assistance in ye obtaining these Somer Assizes the mannagement whereof wee shall wholly leave to your honor Submitting our selves to what in your wisdome shall bee thought most expedient in ye condicon att present our Towne is in, a particular whereof wee are now this bold to trouble you with, the truth whereof is attested by us who are your Honors most obliged servants,

W ... Amett Tho. Ethersey
George Carter Henry Robinson
Tho. Hillesdon Nathan Kent
Tho. Mason Hugh Ethersey
Oliver Pashlar, vicar[3]

The reference to 'a tenant in one part of his house' suggests that, even at this date, Castle House was divided into two, and that John Rogers probably let out the east wing to another family.

Castle House was to remain John Rogers' chief residence until about 1704. But would he be able to rise further in the world – to become not just a gentleman but a landed gentleman too? In 1687 John Rogers married Martha Bridger at Buckingham. His second wife may have come with a useful dowry, for John Rogers was later able to acquire part of the manor of Lenborough, a large hamlet to the south of Buckingham. Lenborough had once been the home of the Ingoldsby family, who were prominent supporters of the Parliamentary cause during the Civil War. Francis Ingoldsby, however, ran through the family fortune and died in the Charter House in 1681. The Lenborough estate was taken over by the Ingoldbys' steward, William Robinson. This William Robinson of Lenborough, gentleman, died in 1697.[4] The estate was then sold by his kinsman, William Robinson of Westminster, to John Rogers of Buckingham. This purchase must have raised John Rogers even further in county society, as he became High Sheriff of Buckinghamshire in 1697. John Rogers was able to purchase another part of Lenborough from John Dormer of Rowsham, Oxfordshire in 1704.

Around 1704, John Rogers left Castle House and moved to Lenborough.[5] He would have lived in the old manor house of the Ingoldsbys, but this may have been in poor condition, as the next owner, Edward Gibbon (grandfather of the historian), demolished it and retained only a modest two-storey house. This reduced house is still standing and comprises five bays, with dormer windows to the attics. It may be that some of the materials from the old manor house had already found their way to Castle House, which was refronted by John Rogers' son, Mathias, in 1708.

John Rogers' generosity ensured that his children all made good marriages. Mathias Rogers married Elizabeth Addington in London in 1709. Her father must have driven a hard bargain for, according to the terms of their marriage settlement, if Mathias and Elizabeth Rogers had no children, then Castle House would descend to the Addington family. John Rogers' daughter Elizabeth married William Streatfeild, citizen and haberdasher of London in 1708. Elizabeth's marriage portion was a farmstead called Rowley House, Lenborough, with four closes of land at Rowley Hill extending to 104 acres.[6] John Rogers' daughter Ann married a John Mingay. Their marriage settlement is mentioned in John Rogers' will of 1722. His younger daughter Martha married Shuckborough Syll of Castlethorp, gentleman, in 1709. Martha's marriage portion was £500. In addition, John Rogers in his will of 1722 left Shuckborough and Martha Sill his interest in the *White Hart Inn* in Newport Pagnell. Their child Elizabeth Sill, baptised at Castlethorp in 1726, was to inherit a life interest in Castle House in the will of John Rogers' son, Mathias Rogers.

John Rogers of Lenborough moved in the highest circles of Buckinghamshire society and evidently played a part in the election of John Verney, Lord Fermanagh, as Knight of the Shire in 1710. William Lowndes wrote to Lord Fermanagh in November 1710 on behalf of Mr Mathias Rogers, reminding him of the services rendered by his father in the election, and fearing that he may be 'removed' in consequence.[7] This may be a reference to John Rogers' position as a burgess in Buckingham, which would be under threat if Sir Richard Temple of Stowe, proprietor of the Borough of Buckingham, knew that he had supported Lord Fermanagh. John Rogers reputation in Buckingham was not unduly affected, as he became Bailiff of the Borough in 1718.

John Rogers of Lenborough, his son Mathias Rogers and William Lowndes were party to a deed regarding the site of the manor house of Lenborough in 1715.[8] According to Browne Willis, however, John Rogers sold his estate at Lenborough in 1718 to Edward Gibbon, a London financier, who was a director of the infamous South Sea Company.[9] John or Mathias Rogers must have retained some land in Lenborough, albeit on lease, because John Rogers continued to live there until his death in 1727.

The move to Lenborough may suggest that John Rogers junior was aspiring to be a 'real' landed gentleman. But, if so, then logically he should have tried to 'plan' a future for his family, to take his descendants ever higher – to knighthoods, baronetcies and, perhaps one day, even to the nobility itself. There were some, rather higher in the social order than the Rogers family, who planned the rise of their houses with almost brutal logic. Among them were the Verneys of Claydon. But the price was high – meagre dowries and legacies for daughters and virtually everything to the oldest son, who would have to marry an heiress regardless of his, or her, inclinations. Nothing could be further from the style of the Rogers: all children are well provided for, daughters have good legacies or dowries, and – as with John Rogers junior himself in 1681 – the eldest son almost seems to lose out.

We must ask why. It could be just a matter of personalities. John Rogers senior and John Rogers junior may have genuinely loved all members of their family and wanted to provide for them properly. It is not easy to get much idea of the real personalities of most of the owners of Castle House. But surviving documents suggest that John Rogers junior was a rather decent man. He certainly displayed a strong sense of responsibility to other members of the family. But it is also possible that he came to recognise that the chances of his family rising further in the world were not all that good and hence concluded there was little point in trying.

The first problem was Castle House itself. While this may have represented the pinnacle of ambition for John Rogers senior, his son should have realised that it was not a good 'launching pad' for further advancement. The problem concerned the location, once one of the greatest advantages. In the past, knights and other important people had been happy to live in the middle of a village or market town. Late medieval and Tudor manor houses tend to be 'on the street', just like Castle House. In the last resort, the owners of such houses saw themselves as part of the community, or, to use the jargon of sociology, of the *gemeinschaft*. Now, those with serious aspirations to grandeur wanted to break their links with the rest of the community and to live apart from it. That meant a house some way outside the town or village, and preferably surrounded by a large park with a high wall. We think of Lord Cobham who, according to (inaccurate) legend, found the proximity of his social inferiors, the villagers of Stowe, so disgusting and intolerable that he demolished the old village and removed the villagers to Dadford so that they could no longer spoil his view. But such drastic 'social engineering' would have been impossible around Castle House. You might be able to demolish Stowe but you could not demolish Buckingham. Although on the edge of the town, Castle House was too much part of it to fit the new ideal. It is surely significant that while several members of the Fowler family had been knights, Lady Richardson had been the last owner to have a title – although there was to be one more titled tenant. There were certainly no more royal visits after 1644.

Perhaps this calculation explains the purchase of Lenborough and the move there in 1704. Lenborough, properly rebuilt and developed, might have fitted the new ideal rather better. But, as we have seen, Rogers 'gave up' on Lenborough when he sold it to Edward Gibbon in 1718. In reality, there was an even bigger problem than the location of Castle House if Rogers really wanted his family to rise further in society: there was actually very little 'opening' for 'landed gentlemen' in the Buckingham area. In fact, this class seemed to be disappearing. The family at Stowe, the Temples, and their successors, the Grenvilles, wanted to buy up virtually every acre that came on the market. Quite often they were prepared to pay over the odds and they usually had longer purses than anyone else. The result of this successful Stowe campaign was that a huge gulf was opening up between the Temple/Grenville family and the next level of society. Perhaps the sale of Lenborough represents a realisation that the transition to true landed gentleman status was virtually impossible.

But it is more likely that John Rogers junior, much less his father, never seriously considered moving up in this way. Their 'inheritance strategy', almost amounting to 'partible inheritance' – as opposed to the 'eldest son takes all' line pursued by the Verneys and essential to serious social advancement – was common in merchant circles, especially with City families. Perhaps the Rogers family were just following the practice of their many London friends and contacts. But, if they did reflect for a while, they would have realised that it made good sense for men in their position.

A degree of 'partible inheritance' fitted well if success in business, not grand titles or status, was the chief objective. Generous provision for daughters and younger sons may not have been entirely altruistic. As we have seen in the case of John Rogers junior's half-sisters, it facilitated good marriages with other merchants and traders. In the days before modern companies the basis of any extended business was partnership and there was likely to be more trust and confidence in partners who were family members.

From the surviving documents we can piece together what was probably the structure of a business system that centred upon beer. Like many country gentlemen, John Rogers junior would have been a maltster as well as a farmer. The farm at Lenborough probably included a malting and the buildings to the west of Castle House certainly included a malting in 1715. It was natural for John Rogers junior to trade with his brother-in-law, John Gore, the London brewer. He probably also traded with his other brothers-in-law, John Sindry and John Russell. But the half-brothers were also involved. Edward Rogers may have lived in his father's house in Buckingham for a while and should have inherited it on the death of his mother in 1708. By 1711, however, he was in business as a merchant at Baldock in Hertfordshire. We do not know what Edward Rogers of Baldock traded in, but it was probably in grain, or more specifically in barley. The land around Baldock grows what is probably the best barley in England – again pointing to a likely connection with beer. John Rogers senior's younger sons, James and William Rogers, were also merchants, trading at Goodrich, in far-off Pembrokeshire. A base in Pembrokeshire suggests trade with Ireland, which was beginning to export increasing amounts of grain. The three younger sons may have been in business together. In March 1711 they joined in a sale to their brother-in-law, John Sindry, of their respective sixth shares in the Castle Hill.[10] Edward Rogers was back in Buckingham by 1718 when he insured his dwelling house there with the Sun Insurance Company. The policy was issued by a Sun Insurance agent, William Sindry, cheesemonger, of Snow Hill, London, and almost certainly a relative.[11]

Rebuilding Castle House

The interlocking patterns of trade, based on grain and beer, and involving brothers and brothers-in-law, seems to have been lucrative. England was at war and in wartime grain prices were always high. There was also a prospect of government contracts, and Sir George Gore could have been very useful here. By the early years of the 18th century, all the signs are that the Rogers family were doing very well indeed. When John Rogers moved to Lenborough around 1704, his oldest surviving son and heir, Mathias Rogers, a young man who obviously had plenty of money, took over. Mathias was born in Buckingham, presumably at Castle House, in 1683. He married Elizabeth Addington, daughter of William Addington, at St Benet Pauls Wharf, London, in 1709. The marriage settlement is referred to in Mathias Rogers' will of 1753 and could well have brought new wealth to the family. Although Browne Willis states that it was in 1708 that Mathias Rogers rebuilt the south wing of Castle House, building projects of this scale are rarely completed on schedule and 1708 may only have been an approximation. It is more likely to have been Mathias Rogers' marriage in 1709 that prompted the modernisation of Castle House. Some ninety years had elapsed since the great rebuilding undertaken by William Lambert and tastes had changed once more. If Mathias Rogers was to please his wife and gain acceptance into the circle of the 'county gentry', he would have to change the largely Jacobean appearance of his house. It was Mathias Rogers who was responsible for giving Castle House the appearance it presents on West Street to this day. Perhaps the best way to describe the transformation is to quote the words of Nikolaus Pevsner:

> Further on, still on the N side, Castle House, by far the most important house in the town. The south front is of 1708, very stately. Eight bays and two storeys, with a four-bay centre and somewhat projecting two-bay wings. Brick and stone dressings. Quoins, good window surrounds, hipped roof with rectangular chimneystacks, margined with stone, and the steep dormers used some fifty years earlier, the middle one with a curious hood. The centre is of four bays, so that the doorway could be placed centrally. It is tall and has a segmental pediment high up. This is, for symmetry's sake, repeated in the adjoining window. This Queen Anne facade belongs to the rebuilt south range of a pre-Reformation courtyard house.[12]

Pevsner notes the extra door case in the four-bay centre and attributes this to a desire for symmetry. Another interpretation could be that Mathias Rogers provided two entrances for two separate suites of rooms, either for two branches of the Rogers family, or for their tenants. After all, there had been a tenant in part of the house in 1684, well before the rebuilding, and, as we shall see, a tenant was sharing the premises in 1725.

Did Mathias Rogers have any specific ideas about what he wanted? Could he have said to his builder, 'Make my house like so and so'? Perhaps he did. There is a slight similarity between the new south front and another grand brick house – like Castle House, on the edge of a built-up area – only a few miles from Buckingham. Perhaps Mathias Rogers wanted something like Winslow Hall – and, as we have seen, John Rogers junior had business dealings with its owners, the Lowndes family. Of course, Castle House is not really like Winslow Hall; in many ways it is much nicer. All of Winslow Hall was built at the same time and its architecture is uniform and homogenous. For us, one of the greatest delights of Castle House is its lack of uniformity. All around us we can see the distinctive architectural contributions from the different stages of its development – everything from the medieval period to the Victorian age and later. But it was only in the 19th century that such diversity came to be appreciated as giving a house greater charm and appeal. In Mathias Rogers' time uniformity was all the rage; in all probability he would have been rather embarrassed by the surviving Jacobean and medieval parts of his house. Given a free hand, the chances are that he would have preferred to get rid of them and rebuild Castle House in its entirety.

Family Crises

But Mathias did not have a free hand. The building work went no further than the south front and the earlier parts of the house survived. We should be grateful for that. The Rogers family must have been riding high when the work commenced, but the fact that things were not taken further suggests that the money ran out, that in 1711 or thereabouts the family faced a serious crisis. While there are many things about Castle House and its owners that must be left to guesswork, the crisis facing the Rogers family was very real and is quite well documented.

20   The new front of Castle House, built by Mathias Rogers in 1708.

As we have seen, John Rogers junior probably traded extensively with his half-brothers and brothers-in-law. A system of trade based on family links has many good features. But it is never wholly secure and carries one enormous danger. What will happen if one of those links proves incompetent, dishonest or is just plain unlucky? Will he drag down the rest and destroy the entire family fortune? The reason why the work at Castle House stopped must surely be because John Gore, brewer of London, husband of John Rogers' half-sister, Martha, was declared bankrupt in 1711. At times like these a steady nerve and family solidarity were more important than ever. It must be said that John Rogers junior, Mathias' father, behaved admirably, but he would surely have insisted that the expensive building work should cease and may have even expected Mathias to put in some of his own money to help in a time of crisis. John Rogers junior and his son, with his wife's substantial dowry behind him, were probably never in serious danger, but a period of restraint was probably called for.

John Rogers junior agreed to pay 5s. in the pound to Gore's creditors. He also agreed with Gore's assignees in bankruptcy, John Harkness and George Brough of London, to pay £60 to redeem the sixth part of the Castle Hill which Gore had in right of his wife, Martha. As with many bankrupts, Gore bounced back. In 1713 he raised a £300 mortgage from William Knight of London enabling him to buy back his share of Castle Hill from John Rogers and to purchase another sixth share belonging to John and Anne Russell. But, even if things were looking up, work at Castle House was not resumed.

Sadly, there are signs that the period of caution did not last long enough. All would probably have been well if the family had stuck to grain and beer – fundamentally sound and profitable businesses. In 1717 they began a series of sales, not it seems to meet any pressing liabilities, but rather to realise assets to invest in what promised to be more lucrative ventures. In 1717, Gore joined with his brother-in-law, John Sindry, in selling the entirety of Castle Hill to George Bridger of London, victualler – almost certainly a relation of John Rogers junior's second wife – for a total of £532. It was Bridger's son, another George Bridger, who sold Castle Hill to Lord Verney in 1762.[13] As we have seen, in 1718 John Rogers junior sold Lenborough to Edward Gibbon.

As with the transfer of Castle House from the Bagots to the Monteages in 1667, we must think about these sales more carefully. It has to be admitted that there has been an element of speculation in our identification of the Rogers fortune with grain and beer – although the circumstantial evidence seems strong. Here we become rather more speculative. What is the most likely explanation for the flurry of land sales in 1717 and 1718? They may have been prompted by the need to clear off debt hanging over from the crisis of 1711. But the time lag looks too long and, in any case, there are signs of recovery in the last few years. Let us suppose, however, that, conscious of advancing years, John Rogers junior and his brothers-in-law decided that that they wanted to get really rich quickly to secure the futures of their wives and children before it was too late. Beer and malting were all very well in their way, but they were not very glamorous; the business required much personal attention and growing amounts of capital investment as plant became more sophisticated. What was needed was something that would bring massive profits without any serious personal effort on the part of the investor.

At the same time, of course, it needed to be safe. The ideal was an investment where, as the saying goes, 'you just cannot lose'. Painful experience over the centuries should have taught investors that ventures that promise incredible profits without any risk are as rare as hens' teeth – in other words, they exhibit the now familiar phenomenon of a stock market 'mania' followed by the inevitable 'bust'. By the time of the land sales of 1717 and 1718, the South Sea stock was beginning to rise nicely. But is there any reason to link Rogers and his family with the South Sea Company and the 'Bubble'? The clue is to be found in the Lenborough sale. The purchaser, Edward Gibbon, was one of the leading lights in the Company, a man skilled in promoting the sale of its shares as a sure way to wealth beyond the dreams of avarice. If Gibbon and Rogers met, Gibbon would have probably said something like, 'Now, Mr Rogers, if you are really wise, why don't you allow me to pay for your estate in South Sea Stock? I tell, you, Sir, you'll double, nay quadruple, your money in no time.' And Gibbon was probably not the only one who gave this advice. John Gore's cousin, another John Gore, son of the former Lord Mayor, and now a respected financier and wine shipper, was a Governor of the South Sea Company and a major shareholder.[14]

For some time South Sea stock went up and up. It must have been tempting to realise more safe assets to buy more of an investment that could only rise to ever more dizzy heights. Yet the day of reckoning was coming. If Rogers and his relations did invest in the South Sea Company and were still holding its shares when the 'Bubble' burst in the autumn of 1720, they would have suffered tremendous losses. Before long the new owner of Lenborough was under investigation for fraud.

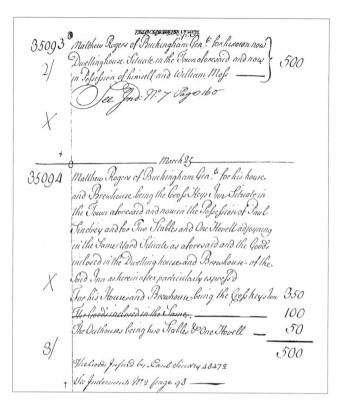

21 Mathias Rogers' Sun Fire Insurance policies for Castle House and the *Cross Keys Inn*, 1725.

Fire and Insurance

While any connection between the Rogers family and the South Sea Bubble is essentially speculative, it is striking that they seem to have made no more purchases of land or other property. The family certainly survived and remained quite wealthy but it looks as if they had risen as far as they would go. In any case, the family – along with much of the rest of Buckingham – soon faced another disaster. In March 1725 a terrible fire broke out in the middle of the town. A strong wind from the east fanned the flames westwards. Parts of Market Hill, Well Street, Castle Street and even the lower end of West Street were destroyed. Some three hundred people were left homeless. Mathias Rogers must have feared for Castle House itself, but the fire stopped before it reached the upper part of West Street and Castle House was safe. The Rogers family was perhaps fortunate, too, in that they had sold their houses around Castle Hill – most of these were destroyed. In any case, Rogers, unlike many of the victims of the fire, was fully covered by fire insurance. There is a surviving Sun Fire Insurance plaque at Castle House bearing the number 5255. This relates to a policy taken out by Mathias Rogers on his own dwelling house in 1715. Another policy covered the contents of the house. In two separate policies taken out at the same time, he insured the malthouse next to his house and all the goods and merchandise in the building. All four policies were issued by a Mr Addington, a Sun Insurance agent living in Cross Lane, near St Mary's Hill, in London. 'Addington' was the maiden name of Mathias Rogers' wife. If the agent was a relative, this might explain why Mathias Rogers was the first man in Buckingham to invest in fire insurance.

Mathias Rogers added to and renewed his fire insurance policies regularly. In 1717 he insured the *Cross Keys Inn*, West Street, then in the tenure of John Ashworth. The *Cross Keys* was one of the largest inns in Buckingham and occupied the entirety of the building now numbered 4-6 West Street.[15] He also insured his property at Lenborough, then occupied by his father, John Rogers.[16] He probably insisted that the overseers also take out fire insurance too, for he and his Poor Law officers insured the parish workhouse in 1718.[17] In 1720 he insured two barns, three stables, two hovels and a cart house adjoining his own house for £300. He even insured his property in Norwich, including the *Castle Inn*, the *Half Moon* and two other houses in the city.[18]

Only days after the fire of Buckingham in 1725, Mathias Rogers amended his insurance policies. He raised the valuation of his own house to £500.[19] Part of the house was in his own occupation, but another part of the building was in the tenure of William Moss, the Independent minister whose Meeting House had been destroyed in the fire. Moss may not have been a tenant for long, for he soon purchased a new plot of land in Well Street and built the Meeting House which survives to this day. Moss died in 1727, soon after the new Meeting House was opened, at the early age of 43.[20] That Mathias Rogers could accommodate William Moss's household, even for a brief period, suggests that the old east wing was let out even at this date. Indeed, the new south wing may well have had two doorways and two halls, providing separate access for two different occupants.

Following the fire, Mathias Rogers also insured two other tenements adjoining his house, then in the occupation of James Southell and William Saul, for £100 each. The insurance extended to his goods in several barns and a woodhouse in his own yard which was evidently approached through a gateway with a roof over it.[21] Mathias Rogers also increased the valuation of the *Cross Keys Inn*, West Street, to £350.[22] His tenant at the inn was then Paul Sindry (almost certainly a relative), who insured the contents of the building with the Sun Insurance Company in 1729.[23] In all, Mathias Rogers took out insurance for £1,150.

In 1727, some two years after the fire, John Rogers junior died at Lenborough. Since he had been born about 1650, he would have been not far off eighty. Unlike his father, whose will had been drawn up hastily immediately before his death, John Rogers junior's will was made in 1722, five years before he died. It is clear that he had already made over a good deal of his property to his son Mathias and to his daughter Ann, wife of John Mingay. His main concern was to leave his property in Newport Pagnell to his daughter Martha and her husband, Shuckborough Syll of Castlethorpe. Martha had already received £500 at the time of her marriage and the Sylls had also been given the rents from the *White Hart Inn*, three tenements and a butcher's shop. But:

> ... now my will is and I do hereby give and devise for the love and affection which I have and bear towards my said son in law Shuckborough Syll and my daughter Martha his now wife unto the said Shuckborough Syll all that house or tenement above mentioned called the White Hart and also all those other three before mentioned tenements situate and being in the yard or backside belonging to the same and likewise all that house and shop now in the tenure of the above mentioned William Harvey ... and also the further sum of five hundred pounds of good and lawful money of Great Britain to have and to hold the aforementioned tenements and premises with their and every of their appurtenances to him the said Shuckborough Syll and his heirs for ever...

John Rogers left a diamond ring, 'now in the keeping of his daughter Martha Syll', to his granddaughter Frances Syll, his gold watch to his granddaughter, and £10 to his maid servant Ann Hawkins. Mathias Rogers and Shuckborough Syll are appointed as executors. Thus John Rogers junior continued the same quite generous provision for daughters characteristic of his father's will some forty years earlier.

Mathias Rogers and Castle House

We noted that, in 1684, it was feared the judges who came to Buckingham to hold the Assizes might be afraid to take up their normal lodgings at the house of John Rogers, because a tenant in part of Rogers' house had suffered from smallpox. At that time the judges may well have found accommodation elsewhere, but they had definitely returned by 1735. Browne Willis states that Mathias Rogers, the 'present possessor' of the house:

> Fronted it Anno 1708 and hath so well fitted up the apartments, and so neatly and elegantly furnished them that the judges on leaving their quarters, at Mr. Mason's, the Recorder's house, and lodging here on their circuits, have acknowledged, that they are in no shire town whatsoever better or more conveniently lodged and accommodated.[24]

Castle House was vital to Browne Willis's sustained campaign to restore Buckingham to its rightful place as the 'Capital of the County'. In particular, he was anxious to ensure that there could be no question that Buckingham would 'lose' the Assizes. Of course, there was the problem of no proper gaol to hold the prisoners awaiting trial. Browne Willis campaigned ceaselessly for such a gaol and his efforts were eventually rewarded with the building of what is now the Old Gaol Museum in 1748 and with the passing of the 'Cobham's Act' of the same year, 'fixing' the Summer Assizes at Buckingham. But, even in 1735, Willis could use the elegance and convenience of Castle House, now at least partially rebuilt, as judges' lodgings to further his case. It is true that Mathias Rogers may have placed his house at the disposal of the judges for nothing, out of a sense of civic duty, but he might have received payment.

It is striking that Mathias Rogers was never Bailiff of Buckingham, as his father and grandfather had been. The Bailiff was expected to entertain lavishly and the absence of Mathias Rogers from the list of bailiffs could suggest a retiring disposition, slightly straitened circumstances or even gentlemanly distaste for the company of Buckingham tradesmen. But Mathias was a Governor of Christ's Hospital. In 1724, together with Charles Blunt, John and Mathias Rogers agreed to lease 'Knights House' in Well Street, a property belonging to the Hospital, to the Overseers of the Poor, for a period of 83 years at a rental of one pound per annum. The Knights House was to be Buckingham's workhouse until the construction of the Union Workhouse in the Stratford Road over a century later.

Mathias and Elizabeth Rogers lived at Castle House from 1709 until his death in 1753. When his father, John Rogers of Lenborough, died in 1727, Mathias Rogers must have inherited some leasehold property in Lenborough. In March 1737 he agreed with the landlord, Nathaniel Primatt of St Biddulph without Aldersgate, chemist, to renew his lease on the Lenborough estate for a further 21 years at a heavy annual rent of £360. This certainly does not suggest poverty. The land included the Windmill Field, then divided into four, Marsh Meadow, The Park,

Penn Leas, Great Rymehill and Rynehill Meadow. In the same year, he agreed to build a new dairy house at Great Rynehill at a cost of £200, and was allowed to withhold £200 of his annual rent. Nathaniel Primatt sold the Lenborough property to Ralph Earl Verney in 1744. [25]

On occasion, Mathias Rogers may have lived at Lenborough in preference to Castle House. Ralph Verney, writing to his father in January 1742, states:

> Mr Rogers of Lethernborough came to dinner here to tell me of a scheme for reducing the poor rate at Buckingham which is grown very high. They have a workhouse at Buckingham but the poor are never employed in it. They designed now, if they can raise a stock of money, to set up proper tools in the workhouse for making sailcloth and sacking, and by this means they will this next year reduce about one third of the rate. They propose to get £100 of each member and that every gentleman who has an estate in the parish shall subscribe to it in proportion to his estate, mr Rogers says they will all come into it. They have agreed with a master workman to undertake it. [26]

As Mathias and Elizabeth Rogers had no children, they were able to offer a home at Castle House to their niece Elizabeth Syll, daughter of Shuckborough and Martha Syll, who was baptised at Castlethorpe in 1726.

The End of the Rogers Era

Mathias Rogers of the Town of Buckingham gentleman made his will on 20 June 1751. It is very long, but in essence he follows the terms of his own marriage settlement in leaving life interests in his property to his wife Elizabeth and his niece, Elizabeth Syll, with Castle House ultimately descending to William Addington, eldest son of his brother-in-law, John Addington. The actual wording is as follows:

> Whereas by my marriage articles and other good and sufficient conveyances and assurances in the law all my freehold messuages lands tenements tithes and hereditaments situate lying or being in the parish of Buckingham aforesaid (except such as I have acquired or purchased since my marriage) are settled or thereby intended to be settled upon my said wife Elizabeth Rogers for and during the term of her natural life as and for her jointure or in part of her jointure … and from and after the determination of my said wife's estate therein …. To the use of my Niece Elizabeth Sill youngest daughter of my late sister Martha Syll deceased for the term of her natural life … brothers in law John Addington of the City of London merchant and Charles Addington of Litchborough in the County of Northampton clerk … Nephew in law William Addington eldest son of my said brother in law John Addington.

Mathias Rogers left an annuity of £40 to Elizabeth Syll in addition to her life interest in Castle House, but stipulated that his wife Elizabeth must approve of any marriage entered into by his niece. This approval must have been given, for Elizabeth Syll did indeed marry before her aunt died.

The extent of Mathias Rogers' property is remarkable, given the fluctuations in the family fortunes we have observed. Apart from Castle House and the *Cross Keys Inn*, he still held the lease of the house and land at Lenborough, he retained property in Newport Pagnell, and he still owned several houses in the parish of St Peter Mancroft in the City of Norwich. He made careful provision for the family heirlooms:

> I give and bequeath unto my said brothers in law the said John Addington and
> Charles Addington all my household goods household furniture linen woolen
> pewter brass pictures china ware plate brewing vessels and implements of household
> whatsoever which shall be about my now dwelling house at Buckingham aforesaid
> and outhouses thereto belonging at the time of my death upon trust nevertheless
> to permit and suffer the same to continue and remain as heirlooms in and about
> my said house for the use of my said wife during her life and after her decease
> for the use of all and every such person and persons who for the time being
> shall respectively be seized or possessed of the freehold of the same house and
> premises … I will that an inventory shall be taken thereof as soon as conveniently
> may be after my death and deposited with my said trustees.

The witnesses to Mathias Rogers' will were his servant, Elizabeth Goldby, and John
Miller 'clerk to Mr Land'. John Land of Buckingham, attorney, was to become the
tenant of Castle House after Rogers' death. John Land also acted for the Purefoys of
Shalstone. He died in 1762, leaving his law books to his nephew, John Miller. John
Miller was succeeded by his son, Ralph Miller, whose son Robert Miller continued
the family legal firm in Buckingham until his death in 1817. Mathias Rogers died,
aged 70, in 1753. He was survived by his wife, Elizabeth Rogers, who made her
own will on 6 May 1754:

> I give to nephew Mr William Addington of London, son of my brother Mr
> John Addington, the sum of twenty guineas to buy him mourning And as to
> for and concerning all the rest and residue of ready money and all my securities
> for money household goods and furniture plate rings jewels cattle corn grain
> hay malt implements of husbandry arrears of rent right credits chattels personal
> estate and effects whatsoever and wheresoever and of what nature kind or quality
> soever the same may be which I have any power to dispose of (after payment
> of my debts and funeral expenses) I give and bequeath the same and every part
> hereof unto my dear and affectionate niece Elizabeth Sill who now lives with
> me her executors administrators and assigns to and for her and their own sole
> and proper use and benefit free from any claims or demands of any other of
> my relations or other persons whatsoever of in to or out of the same And I do
> hereby make constitute and appoint my said niece Elizabeth Sill full and sole
> executrix of this my last will and testament.

As we have seen, Mathias and Elizabeth Rogers had no children and hence the
direct Rogers line became extinct. We see here the significance of the provision in
the marriage settlement of Mathias and Elizabeth Rogers that, if the couple had no
children, Castle House should pass to the Addington family. The settlement effectively
precluded the house passing to any of the male descendants of John Rogers junior's
half-brothers – who would normally have been regarded as the next heirs.

Absentees and Tenants

The problem for the Addingtons of a long wait for the life interests in Castle House
to expire was solved when John Addington married Elizabeth Syll at Buckingham on
7 April 1755. With the death of Elizabeth Rogers in 1756, Castle House would have
become vacant, but the couple decided against living at Buckingham. In other words,
Castle House was not only passing out of the Rogers family but its ownership was
also passing out of Buckingham. Castle House was evidently tenanted by 1757, when
John Addington of Mincing Lane, London, packer, insured his newly acquired property

in Buckingham. [27] The Sun Insurance plaque, number 154580, still survives at Castle House. The details of the insured property are as follows:

One house only in the tenure of John Land & Thomas Theed stone brick & tiled	500
Household goods therein only the property of Mr Addington	100
Malthouse only in the yard stone brick & tiled	300
Two stables only adjoining stone & tiled	50
Great barn only stone & thatched	50
On the dwelling house only of the Cross Keys Inn brick & tiled	
In the tenure of innholder	300
Brewhouse only adjoining brick timber & tiled	100
Six bays of stabling in one building brick timber & tiled	100
	1500

This shows that Castle House, still valued at £500, was in the occupation of John Land, the attorney, and Thomas Theed, a well-to-do Buckingham farmer. Later deeds to Castle House show that Theed had been tenant of some of the farmland attached to Castle House even in the time of Mathias Rogers.

The heir to Castle House, William Addington, lived in London, where his daughter, Wilhelmina Caroline, was baptised in 1756. William Addington, then of St George's, Bloomsbury, gentleman, died in 1779. He left estates at Henhurst in Surrey, Romford in Essex and in the Town of Buckingham to his wife Caroline for life, with remainder to his brother John Addington. Although he made generous bequests to other members of his family, he refrained from giving a legacy to his mother-in-law, Mrs Arnold, 'whose considerable fortune places her superior to any little offers from me makes me to request her to accept of a ring value two hundred pounds as a remembrance of my affection'. William Addington's property in Buckingham in fact passed to his daughter Wilhelmina Caroline, wife of James Hatch, of Oldford, Middlesex, malt distiller.

James Hatch insured his property in Buckingham with the Royal Insurance Company in 1780:

James Hatch of the Town & County of Buckingham Esq	
On a house brewhouse & stables adjoining in the tenure of	
Thomas Ayres an innholder known by the sign of the Cross Keys	600
On a house situate in Horn Street late in the occupation	
of Shillingford but now empty	400
On a house washhouse barn malthouse stables & offices adjoining	
Brick stone timber built & tiled & thatched in the	
tenure of Thomas Theed farmer & maltster	1000
On houses adjoining stone built & thatched in the tenure	
of Messrs Jones & Philips not exceeding £40 each	80
On a house adjoining in the tenure of John Bull	40
On a house adjoining in the tenure of James Gregory	50
On a house adjoining in the tenure of John Jones	20
On a house adjoining in the tenure of Henry Holt	20
On two houses adjoining brick & stone built & thatched in	
the tenure of Messrs Meads & Smith not exceeding £20 each	40
On a house situate in Well Street in the tenure of Judith Clarke	20
	2,270[28]

According to the valuation agreed with the Royal Insurance Company, Castle House, with its barn and malthouse, now occupied by Thomas Theed, was worth £1,000. The nearby *Cross Keys Inn*, in the occupation of Thomas Ayres, was worth £600. These valuable properties were sold by James Hatch to the sitting tenant, Thomas Theed of Buckingham, farmer and maltster, in 1782.

After the deaths of Mathias and Elizabeth Rogers, the status of Castle House probably declined. The Buckingham area was now almost totally dominated by the owner of Stowe – soon to be a Duke. No resident of Castle House, however grand, could really hope to be treated as the equal of a Duke. There were only two courses open: one was to accept Stowe's supremacy and to seek to profit from it by the provision of professional or commercial services; the other way was to challenge Stowe, if only indirectly. There was only one local family capable of offering any serious resistance to the dominance of Stowe and they were the Verneys of Claydon. The owner of Castle House might align himself with the Verneys and use Castle House as a 'stalking horse' for Verney influence in the town. Such a course was dangerous but it might pay social or business dividends. As we shall see, the strategy varied from time to time. The Boxes were to ally with Stowe and the Hearns with Claydon. But, either way, the role of Castle House, while still important, would be secondary in the wider contest for power. There are a number of curious ambiguities about Castle House. As we have seen, it was on the 'frontier' between the town of Buckingham and the countryside; in the last resort it was a 'country house' within the boundaries of a town. So, too, especially in the 18th and 19th centuries, Castle House was on another frontier – the imprecise social boundary between the sphere of the gentry proper and the more workaday world of business and the professions.

Chapter Six

THE THEEDS AND SHILLINGFORDS:
GENTLEMEN FARMERS

The Theeds

In February 1782 James Hatch and his wife, Wilhelmina Caroline, sold Castle House to Thomas Theed of Buckingham Esq. for the sum of £2,000.[1] The sale included the *Cross Keys Inn*, West Street, and land to the north of Castle House. The Royal Insurance policies suggest that Thomas Theed had rented part or all of Castle House at least since 1757. As sitting tenant, he should have been able to buy Castle House for a relatively modest sum, although the large profit apparently made by the Theed family when they sold Castle House only two years later, in 1784, may also reflect the value of other land and tithes in Buckingham which they already owned before 1782.

Thomas Theed had become a burgess of Buckingham on 21 June 1779. On 14 January 1783, with the other burgesses, he signed a document appointing the Hon. William Wyndham Grenville as one of the Principal Burgesses. Thomas Theed features on the land tax returns for the Borough of Buckingham in 1783. His main payment of £5 15s. 5d. must be for Castle House and the land which went with it. His property, tenants and assessments were as follows:

Mr Theed:	John Gregory	0	1	10
	Mr Coffee	0	1	10
	Late Jones	0	1	10
	Joseph Phillips	0	1	10
	Mr Theed for Hillesden	0	3	4
	Do for Page Hill	0	6	9
	Do	5	15	5
	Do for malting	0	3	4
	Mr Theed			
	Mr Ayres	0	5	2
	Cross Keys	1	11	0

Thomas Theed made his will on 3 September 1782, the year in which he bought Castle House. He left an annuity of £20 to his sister Finetta Theed, charged on his estate at Thornborough, which was left to his nephew John Theed, son of his brother John Theed. His main bequest, including the newly purchased Castle House, was also to the same nephew:

> I give and devise all and every my freehold and copyhold messuages cottages closes lands tenements tithes and hereditaments situate and being in town fields parish and precincts of Buckingham aforesaid together with all and singular the appurtenances thereto respectively belonging or appertaining and all my estate right title and interest therein unto the use of my said nephew, John Theed.

Thomas Theed left several legacies, including £100 to his brother John Theed and £500 to his nephew Thomas Theed. Thomas Theed the testator was evidently related to Mrs Penelope Smith, of Buckingham, widow. He mentions her son, Mr John Smith, and her granddaughter, Penelope, daughter of Henry Smith, late of Bicester, gentleman. Penelope Smith will appear in the next chapter, for she married Philip Box, nephew of Philip Box the banker, a subsequent owner of Castle House.

Thomas Theed appointed his nephew John Theed as his only executor. He died in 1783 or in early 1784. His heir, John Theed, was a London haberdasher who seems to have died young. In 1793 his father, John Theed, was granted letters of administration of the goods and chattels of Thomas Theed of Buckingham deceased, left unadministered by John Theed, the sole executor and residuary legatee. On 15 September 1784 John Theed, haberdasher of Philpot Lane, London, sold Castle House to Farmer Shillingford of Hillesden, Gentleman, for the sum of £3,350–£1,350 more than the purchase price in 1782.[2]

The Shillingfords

The Shillingfords had been tenant farmers at Padbury from at least 1670. John Shillingford of Padbury signed the Oath of Allegiance in 1723. Richard Shillingford married Dorothy Farmer in London in 1726. Their son, Farmer Shillingford, was born in Buckingham in 1731, and married Elizabeth Devonshire at South Mimms in 1754. Farmer Shillingford's sister, Hannah, married William Andrewes, a barrister-at-law, in 1750. In the 19th century the Andrewes family were to hold the lease of the All Souls manor in Maids Moreton and built the big Victorian house called Southfield, later known as The Manor. Thomas, the only son of Farmer and Elizabeth Shillingford, was baptised at South Mimms in 1759. A daughter, also Elizabeth, was married at Hillesden in 1782 to William Gurden, a lace dealer of Towcester. After the death of his first wife, Farmer Shillingford married Ann, widow of Benjamin Price Withers, lord of the manor of Westbury, Buckinghamshire.

Castle House is not mentioned by name in the 1784 conveyance to Farmer Shillingford, but is described as follows:

> All that capital messuage or tenement situate lying and being in the Town of Buckingham aforesaid in a certain street there called West Street alias Fowler Street late in the tenure of the said Thomas Theed together with the malt kiln, dove house, wheat house, brew house, working floor, cistern, yards, cherry orchard, gardens and backsides to the said messuage or tenement belonging.

A cottage, probably part of the buildings to the west of the house is next described: 'And also all that cottage adjoining to the said brew house now or late in the occupation of Anne Grace'.

A more substantial house is also described and appears to be the east wing of Castle House; Farmer Shillingford, the purchaser in 1784, is given as a former tenant of this semi-detached property: 'And all that messuage or tenement with the garden stable and appurtenances thereto belonging formerly part of the said capital messuage and situate in the Town of Buckingham aforesaid formerly in the tenure of the said Farmer Shillingford and now of Richard Smith.' The right of way over the fields to the Conduit House erected by the Lamberts is still carefully specified:

Together with liberty of way or passage in the usual and customary manner as hitherto enjoyed by the said Thomas Theed and those under whom he claimed through certain fields in or near Buckingham aforesaid to a conduit or spring head in a certain field called Conduit Field for amending the pipes or any part of the aqueduct which conveys the water from the said conduit to the said capital messuage without doing any wilful damage to the said grounds or any of the fences thereof and making the same good again by repairing thereof.

Amongst the land conveyed to Farmer Shillingford with Castle House were several closes of land to the north of Castle House:

All those several closes or inclosed grounds and pieces of arable land late in the occupation of the said Thomas Theed lying in the parish of Buckingham aforesaid northward of the said capital messuage and to the same belonging heretofore in the possession of Mathias and Elizabeth Rogers and late in the possession of the said Thomas Theed and hereinafter particularly mentioned that is to say
All that close called the House Close containing 3 acres and 2 roods,
All that close called Cow Pasture Close or Milking Ground containing 4 acres 2 roods and 23 poles or perches,
All that close called Drewfield or Dreyfield containing 8 acres 2 roods and 11 poles or perches,
All that close called the Pit Close containing about two acres ...
All that piece of arable land called the Ten Acre Piece lying in the parish of Buckingham or Maids Moreton Field and containing about 7 acres 2 roods and 24 poles or perches and ten acres of arable in the North Field of Buckingham.

The property conveyed also included five other houses:

Two of them situate in West Street alias Fowlers Street aforesaid and were now or late in the tenure or occupation of William Coffery and John Gregory
Two others of them situate in Saint Rumbalds Lane and in the tenure of William Hill and William Cross
And the other of them situate on the north side of the Castle Hill and in the tenure of John Jones and Ann Holt.

Another significant property conveyed to Farmer Shillingford was

All that messuage or inn situate in the town of Buckingham aforesaid and lately called the Cross Keys Inn together with the barns stables outhouses and all and singular the appurtenances thereunto belonging as the same were formerly in the possession of George Little and afterwards of Joseph Woolams Thomas Ayres and Thomas Bennett

The precise location of the *Cross Keys Inn* has long been discussed in Buckingham. The 1784 conveyance gives a very precise description of a separate stable and granary near to and used with the *Cross Keys Inn*. The stable was:

Situate lying and being in the Town of Buckingham aforesaid in the aforesaid street there called West Street or Fowlers Street the premises formerly of Mrs Playdell and since of Richard Watts towards the west the garden and barn formerly of William Alton and the garden ground formerly of Sir Richard Temple and the Cross Keys Inn aforesaid toward the east and the orchard formerly of said William Alton and afterwards of William Turpin towards the north and the said street called the West Street or Fowlers Street towards the south.

Thus the *Cross Keys*, the emblem of St Peter, one of the two patrons of Buckingham church, was clearly on the north side of West Street. The present buildings on that side of the street are little altered since 1784, and the obvious candidate for the *Cross Keys Inn* is the elegant range now numbered 4-6 West Street. This building has two blocked archways that could have been entries to a coach and stable yard for a substantial inn. It is significant that successive owners of Castle House, including Mathias Rogers, Thomas Theed and Farmer Shillingford, were all maltsters, with a ready outlet for their product in the *Cross Keys Inn*, one of Buckingham's leading coaching inns.

The 1784 conveyance also shows that Thomas Theed had an early interest in the land belonging to Castle House, having collected tithes due to Mathias Rogers, William Addington, and later to James Hatch. Farmer Shillingford's purchase included

> And all such tithes and tenths of corn grain hay lamb wool and other things yearly arising renewing and increasing in and out of the said lands tenements and hereditaments and some part thereof or any arable lands ley meadow and pasture ground in or near the town of Buckingham aforesaid as had been or usually had and taken by the said Thomas Theed as tenant to the said James Hatch and before him as tenant to the said William Addington and Matthias Rogers deceased and mentioned and described in the schedule or inventory thereof thereon endorsed.

Farmer Shillingford insured Castle House with the Sun Insurance Company in 1785.[3] The valuation was as follows:

	£
Farmer Shillingford of the Town of Buckingham gentleman	
On his now dwelling house and tenement adjoining situate	
as aforesaid brick and tiled except a small part plaster	800
Household goods therein	200
Malthouse granary two stables barns cowhouse gatehouse	
pigsties leantoos all adjoining near tiled and thatched	360
Utensils and stock therein	500
Wheathouse only separate thatched	20
Utensils and stock therein	20
Utensils and stock in rickyard only near	100
Barn only separate stone and tiled	50
Brewhouse and offices only adjoining stone and tiled	50
Two tenements only adjoining near in the tenure of	
Gregory and Coffee private Brick and tiled	60
House brewhouse and stables adjoining at Buckingham	
aforesaid in the tenure of Thomas Bennett carrier brick and tiled	400
Granary only separate	40
Stables and hovels adjoining tiled and thatched and party wall	
between and not communicating	100
	2700

Castle House is here valued at £800, but the associated barns and malthouse are separately valued at £360, showing a net increase in the valuation over James Hatch's policy of 1780. The £500 valuation of the stock in the barns and malthouse suggests that Farmer Shillingford was a maltster on a very large scale. The *Cross Keys Inn*

22   *Cross Keys Inn*, West Street, 1990.

is not mentioned by name but is represented by the £400 valuation of the house and brewhouse in the occupation of Thomas Bennett, carrier.

Farmer Shillingford probably had land in several parishes around Buckingham and may have gained control of some of the land belonging to his second wife, Ann. They were living at Hillesden in 1784, and in 1788, he took on the lease of a messuage and land in Padbury formerly rented from All Souls College by Richard Lee.[4] In 1786 Farmer Shillingford's son, Thomas Shillingford, married Susanna Norton at Buckingham church. The marriage was witnessed by Alexander Norton, who ran one of the largest tanneries in Buckingham. Norton's House survives to this day, on Hunter Street, and the row of cottages behind it is still called Norton's Place.

Improvements and Fall

Farmer Shillingford, his wife Ann and his son Thomas definitely lived at Castle House, as is made clear in Farmer Shillingford's will of 1788:

> Also I give and devise to Ann my dear and loving wife for and during the term of her natural life all that part of my mansion house in Buckingham which is occupied and enjoyed by my son Thomas Shillingford and also all such part of the garden adjoining thereto extending up to the yew hedge as was late in the occupation of Mr Land and my will is that the doorway leading out of my said sons apartment into the hall there shall so soon as conveniently may be stopped up and my will further is that my said wife shall have a free passage through the stone wall that incloses the said garden from the street there and in some part of that end of the house given to her my said wife she shall have free liberty to make a doorway therein with full and free liberty of ingress egress and regress at all times to and from the same without any interruption whatsoever.

The curious stipulation for the construction of a new gateway probably suggests that Farmer Shillingford knew that Ann and her stepson did not get on; this gateway still exists. The son, Thomas Shillingford, was expected to move into the main part of the house. It may be that Thomas Shillingford took this opportunity to modify the house, by converting the second doorway in the south façade into a window, and throwing the two halls into one. The style of the fine staircase in the enlarged hall is surely of late 18th-century date and the panelling and fireplace in the upstairs parlour probably date from this time. The work undertaken by Thomas Shillingford around 1790 represents the biggest change since Mathias Rogers' rebuilding some eighty years earlier. Thomas Shillingford must have either had plenty of money or been rather an extravagant young man.

Thomas Shillingford's newly inherited house, or at least its water supply, is mentioned in the 1791 deed by which Philip Box, the banker, bought the Castle Hill, and land to the west of the town, from the Trustees of Earl Verney. The deed recites the following right of access to the land enjoyed by the owner of Castle House:

> And also save and except such right and usage as hath been heretofore customarily exercised by the owners or occupiers for the time being of a certain messuage or mansion house in Buckingham aforesaid heretofore of Lady Coke and now of Thomas Shillingford to take up repair and lay down pipes for conveying water across certain parts of the lands hereby mentioned and intended to be granted released and confirmed from the Conduit in a certain field there called the Upper Field to the said messuage or mansion house in Buckingham aforesaid.[5]

This deed contains the only reference to Lady Coke having been a tenant of Castle House. Lady Coke was Elizabeth, daughter of George Chamberlayne (afterwards Denton) of Hillesdon. She inherited the Denton estates including Hillesden and the Prebend End of Buckingham. She married Wenman Roberts, nephew of Thomas

23   Hall and staircase, Castle House, 2005.

Coke, Earl of Leicester. When the Earl died without an heir in 1759, Wenman Roberts assumed the name of Coke in order to inherit his uncle's estates. Wenman Roberts died in 1776, leaving his widow Elizabeth Coke in possession of Hillesden and the Prebend End of Buckingham. Elizabeth Lady Coke died in 1810. Her son, Thomas William Coke, sold Hillesden and the Prebend End of Buckingham to the Duke of Buckingham in 1823. Elizabeth Lady Coke could therefore have been the tenant of Castle House between her husband's death in 1776 and sale of the house to Farmer Shillingford in 1784.

Thomas Shillingford farmed on quite a large scale. He not only maintained the land attached to Castle House, but also took on the lease of his father's property in Padbury. In 1791 he took over the lease of another farm at Padbury, formerly occupied by Simon Harris. In the following year he absorbed another Padbury farm previously in the tenure of Matthew Swannell. In 1792 he became the tenant of the elegant manor house and extensive farmland at Padbury owned by All Souls College.[6] He even took on the lease of Padbury Mill in 1793. Perhaps he was expecting to make a good profit when Padbury, like so many other North Buckinghamshire villages before it, enclosed its open fields. His name appears in the printed Padbury Enclosure Act of 1795. He was still occupying a farm in Padbury at the time of the enclosure award in 1796.[7] According to the Posse Comitatus, taken in 1798, Thomas Shillingford had six horses, three wagons and four carts. These were located at Buckingham, not at Padbury, so they were presumably housed in the outbuildings to Castle House.

Thomas Shillingford's stepmother evidently remained at Castle House. The land tax of 1795 lists her tenants in the Borough of Buckingham:

Mrs Shillingford:			
John Gregory	0	1	10
Late Coffee	0	1	10
Late Phillips	0	1	10
Late Jones	0	1	10
Hillsdon Piece	0	3	4
Page Hill	0	6	9
Lands	5	15	5
Late Barnard	0	13	11

The land tax returns show her stepson as owner of the *Crown* and *Cross Keys Inn*:

Thomas Shillingford:				
John Hadland		0	3	8
Thomas Griffiths		0	3	8
Empty		0	3	8
Mr Shillingford				
	Mr Stamp	0	5	2
	Do	1	11	0

Ann Shillingford may have remained a tenant in the east wing of Castle House right up to her death. She was buried at Buckingham in 1808. Indeed, it may have been her unwillingness to move which forced her stepson Thomas Shillingford to delay the sale of Castle House until 1798.

By 1794 Thomas Shillingford and his wife Susannah were short of cash and raised a mortgage on Castle House of £2,000 from Richard Scott of Maids Moreton.[8] But the mortgage from Scott was clearly not enough, for on 3 April 1798 Castle House was sold by auction at the *Cobham Arms Inn* in Buckingham. The principal lot was:

> A capital freehold mansion house, in good condition, and fit for the reception of a genteel family, containing a spacious hall, and stair cases, dining room, three good parlours, ten bedrooms on the first floor, good upper rooms, laundry, brewhouse, stable, and other convenient offices, lately new built, and supplied constantly with water from a conduit, large gardens walled in and well planted with fruit trees, orchards, and two closes of rich pasture land adjoining, containing altogether about 21 acres of ground, situate in (and much detached from) the Town of Buckingham, by the side of the road leading to Stowe, now in the several occupations of Mr Thomas Shillingford and Mrs Bennett.[9]

Some of the other lots are listed here with their tenants and annual rentals:

	£	s.
The Crown Public House let to Mr John Hadland	15	0
A tenement adjoining the Crown, Richard Garratt	4	4
The Cross Keys Public House let to John Coles	6	0
A tenement on Castle Hill, Ezra Hill	2	10
A tenement on Castle Hill, Catherine Bates, widow	1	5
Two freehold tenements on Castle Hill, John Jones, Charles Holt	1	9
Six freehold tenements in the North East End, William Gubbins, Hannah Goode, John Smith, Nicholas Harris, Kinch, Gayton	13	6

The purchaser of the principal lot was Philip Box of Buckingham, banker, who had already snapped up much of the Verneys' property in the town. The surviving abstract of the conveyance does not state how much Philip Box paid for Castle House, but it must have been in excess of £2,000, for Castle House was still mortgaged for that amount to Richard Scott of Maids Moreton. Scott was party to the conveyance of Castle House from Thomas Shillingford and Susannah his wife to Philip Box on 3 May 1798. Thomas Shillingford's brother-in-law, William Gurden of Towcester, was also party to the transaction.[10] It is significant that Philip Box did not purchase the *Cross Keys Inn* at the 1798 sale. He may have thought that the new coaches passing through Stony Stratford, which could reach Birmingham in one day, would put the coaching inns of Buckingham out of business. But, by buying Castle House without the nearby *Cross Keys Inn*, Philip Box was breaking a link between the two properties that had existed for at least 100 years.

Although Philip Box did not buy all the property included in the auction, as the major purchaser he was allotted the deeds to the whole property on completing a deed of covenant for their production whenever the need should arise. This was of particular importance to Thomas Shillingford as several lots in the auction remained unsold. In 1799 Thomas, son of Thomas Shillingford, and Benjamin, son of William Gurden, were each left £100 in the will of Benjamin Price Withers of Westbury. By 1802 Thomas Shillingford had moved to Towcester, the home of his brother-in-law, William Gurden. Gurden's son Benjamin was in fact a godson of Benjamin Price Withers of Westbury. He changed his name to Price in 1808, enabling him to inherit the manor of Westbury.

24   Castle House sale
catalogue, 1798.

PARTICULARS and CONDITIONS of SALE,

OF SUNDRY VALUABLE

Freehold, Copyhold, & Leasehold

ESTATES,

Situate in the Town and Parish of BUCKINGHAM;

WHICH WILL BE

SOLD BY AUCTION,

By *JOHN DAY,*

On TUESDAY the 3d day of APRIL, 1798,

At the *COBHAM ARMS* Inn, in *BUCKINGHAM,*

at TWELVE o'Clock at Noon,

In the following Lots:

LOT I.

A Capital FREEHOLD MANSION HOUSE, in good Condition, and fit
for the Reception of a genteel Family; containing a spacious Hall, and Stair
Cases, Dining Room, three good Parlours, ten Bed Rooms on the first floor,
good upper Rooms, Laundry, Brewhouse, Stable, and other convenient Offices,
lately new built, and supplied constantly with Water from a Conduit, large
Gardens walled in and well planted with Fruit Trees, Orchards, and two Closes
of rich Pasture Land adjoining, containing altogether about twenty-one Acres,
of Ground, situate in (and much detached from) the Town of *Buckingham,* by
the side of the Road leading to *Stowe,* now in the several Occupations of
Mr. THOMAS SHILLINGFORD, and Mrs. BENNETT.   N. B. Immediate
Possession of the greater part of these Premises may be had if required.

*** If thought more desirable the foregoing Lot will be divided into two Lots; the first to
comprise the House and Buildings, Yard, Gardens, Orchards, and adjoining Pasture Ground; the
other to contain the further Close of Pasture Land, adjoining to *Pods Lane* and *Morton Field,* and
called the Pit Close; which latter contains about ten Acres and an half of Ground.

LOT II.

A FREEHOLD TENEMENT, called the *Crown* Public House, in the Town of
Buckingham, let to Mr. John Hadland as Tenant at will, at an under Rent of
15l. per Annum; the House well accustomed, and in compleat Repair, and
one part thereof lately new built.

Lot

Since the sale from James Hatch to the Theeds in 1782, Castle House had changed hands with unusual frequency – to the Shillingfords in 1784 and now in 1798 to Philip Box. The sale to the Shillingfords is easy to understand because the house had passed from a man based in London, and with no obvious interest in Buckingham, to a local gentleman farmer. The sale by the Shillingfords to Box is more interesting. The vendors were clearly in some financial difficulty by 1798. In some ways this is surprising. Farming was doing well in the Revolutionary Wars and the Shillingfords should have been well placed to benefit. But there had been a financial crisis in 1797 and this may have affected the family. As we have seen, however, Thomas Shillingford had taken on a number of tenancies and undertaken major work at Castle House. He could have overstretched himself. In any case, the long-standing link with farming was coming to an end. The Shillingfords were to be the last farmer owners; now it was the turn of bankers, lawyers and finally of brewers once more. Compared with their predecessors and successors, the Theeds and Shillingfords remain somewhat shadowy figures, although Thomas Shillingford's work at Castle House effectively 'finalised' the present arrangements at the front of the house. With the new owners, however, we encounter some rather more rounded characters.

Chapter Seven

THE BOXES:
BANKING AND THE IRISH MYSTERY

THE BOX FAMILY came from Oxfordshire. Philip Box of Bicester, brazier, married Sarah Rainbow at Banbury in 1728. Their eldest son, Edward, was born in Bicester in 1730, and a second son, Philip, in 1740. Philip Box of Bicester, brazier, made his will in 1747, leaving property to his wife, Sarah, his two sons, Edward and Philip, both under 21, and his nephews and nieces, William Minshall, Robert Rainbow Kenning, Thomas Dagnall and Elizabeth Box.

Edward Box of Bourton

Edward, son of Philip Box of Bicester, came to Buckingham about 1752. On 26 October that year he married Ann Jones, daughter of William Jones of Buckingham, grazier, at Stowe church. In 1747 William Jones had taken out a 21-year lease on the farmhouse on the Castle Hill and the 60 acres of land to the west of the town which went with it.[1] William Jones died in 1758, but his wife, Elizabeth Jones, occupied the house on Castle Hill until her death in 1794. By this time Edward Box had taken over the lease on the house, and the freehold had been bought by his brother, Philip Box.[2]

Edward Box must have had other business or family connections in Buckingham. In the will of Acton Chaplin of Buckingham, mercer, dated 27 October 1762, there is a bequest of the large sum of £800 to 'my friend Mr Edward Box of Buckingham aforesaid carrier and his brother Mr Philip Box equally between them'. There is a further reference in the will to a half complete transaction:

> Whereas I have entered into articles of agreement with Mr Edward Box and his brother for the purchase of divers messuages and tenements in Buckingham aforesaid the purchase money for which I have paid now in case of my death before the said purchased premises shall have been conveyed to me I do direct and appoint the same to be conveyed unto the said William Hutton John Whitaker and William Harding.

Edward Box and his wife Anne had four sons, Philip, Edward, Thomas and William. Thomas was baptised at Buckingham in 1768. Edward Box had leased Pound Farm, Bourton, a dairy farm belonging to Ralph Earl Verney.[3] The farm extended to 160 acres, on which Edward Box paid £23 1s. 0d. land tax in 1783. Edward Box had also taken over the lease of the farmhouse on Castle Hill and the 60 acres of land from his mother-in-law, Elizabeth Jones. In 1791 he was paying £100 a year rent for the Castle Hill property.[4] This included the Conduit Close, from where water was conveyed in pipes to Castle House. The conduit may be referred to in a case before the Borough

Quarter Sessions on 4 October 1791: Thomas Steel was sentenced to be whipped for stealing lead piping valued at 10d. 'from the ground of Mr Edward Box, the property of Thomas Shillingford'.[5] Edward Box of Bourton died in 1792, leaving his eldest son, Philip Box, in possession of the Castle Hill, and his son William in control of Pound Farm, Bourton.

Philip Box of Buckingham

Philip Box, the younger son of Philip Box of Bicester, evidently came to Buckingham soon after his brother Edward. Philip Box first appears in the Buckingham records in 1762, having taken over a silk mercer's business formerly owned by Acton Chaplin. Both Philip Box and his brother Edward are mentioned in the will of Acton Chaplin dated 27 October 1762. There is a bequest to 'Mr Philip Box: £10 to buy him mourning'.

Philip Box later branched out to add linen drapery and hosiery to his line of business – very much the same sort of trades that John Rogers had followed a century earlier. He became a Burgess of Buckingham on 3 March 1766 and served as Bailiff in 1767, 1773, 1780, 1788 and 1789. He lived in a large house on the north side of the Market Hill, probably the elegant double-fronted house which was demolished in the 1950s for the building of the Woolworth's store. He also owned a valuable house in Horn or West Street. He insured this property with the Royal Exchange Insurance Company in 1782:

Philip Box of Buckingham mercer	
On his dwelling house situate in the Market Place	500
On household furniture therein	200
On utensils & stock in trade in the same	1200
On a house situate in Horn Street ten	460
On a stable and barn adjoining together & belonging	40
	2400

The said buildings are brick and stone or brick and timber paneled with brick and tiled situate in Buckingham aforesaid.[6]

The insurance valuation of Box's property at £2,400 was only £300 less than that of Farmer Shillingford when he insured Castle House in 1785.

In 1786 Philip Box opened Buckingham's first bank. The bank issued paper notes which were payable at Messrs Praed of Fleet Street, London. Ably supported by his Chief Clerk, George Nelson, Box and his bank prospered and its fortunes were greatly assisted by the business brought by its most important customer, George Nugent Temple Grenville, 2nd Earl Temple and 1st Marquis of Buckingham. The Marquis derived a huge income from his 'sinecure' of Teller of the Exchequer and his banker was admirably placed to make the most of this. The Marquis of Buckingham, who became Lord Lieutenant of Buckinghamshire in 1782, was probably instrumental in securing Box's appointment to the lucrative position of Receiver General of Taxes for the county, and for nominating him to the Commission of Peace. Philip Box would have had to display appropriate deference and employ considerable tact when dealing with the Marquis, who was a notoriously difficult man. Horace Walpole said that he had 'many disgusting qualities, as pride, obstinacy, want of truth, with natural propensity to avarice'.

The Marquis was a leading light in promoting the Parliamentary Act, passed on 30 April 1793, for the building of the Grand Junction Canal, from the Thames at Brentford to Braunston in Northamptonshire. Amongst the sponsors were William Praed of Tyringham, banker, who became the first chairman, Philip Box of Buckingham, who became the treasurer, and Edward Oakley Gray of Buckingham, solicitor, who became one of the company's clerks. In 1801, having formed a new partnership with William Praed, Philip Box arranged that the firm of Box & Praed should be treasurers to the Grand Junction Canal Company.

The only local family capable of challenging the dominance of the mighty Temple-Grenvilles were the Verneys of Claydon. In Box's time, the head of the Verney family was Ralph, Earl Verney and Viscount Fermanagh, who was responsible for the rebuilding of Claydon in at attempt to make it as beautiful as Stowe. But Verney 'dissipated his estates' and is described as 'a man of magnificent instincts, great artistic knowledge and boundless extravagance … He fought the Temples of Stowe and finally came to utter ruin.'[7] By the time of Verney's death, in March 1791, the bailiffs were in possession – all eerily prophetic of Stowe nearly sixty years later. Of course, in life, Box could have had few dealings with the arch-rival of his patron. But, once Verney was dead, he moved swiftly to acquire several houses in Buckingham – almost certainly at a low price – from the Trustees of the Earl's estate. On 25 June 1791 Philip Box paid £2,256 for the Verney property in the town. This comprised:

> The Castle Hill and the houses thereon containing by estimation 8 acres save and excepted only out of this present grant and release so much and such part of the said Castle Hill as was sometime since in the lifetime of the said Ralph Earl Verney granted and conveyed to certain trustees for the purpose of building and erecting thereon a new church there and also so much and such part and parts of the said hill as is contained on the flat or top thereof round the new erected church and as is now in grass upon the slopes or sides thereof including the gardens on the top of the said hill but not extending or including the gardens or ground belonging to or occupied with the cottages there which said several exempted premises as the same hath been recently admeasured staked and set out.

The property also included several closes of land across the river from the Castle Hill:

> Lady's Meadow, 20 acres, occupied by George Little
> Bradbury Close and Bradbury's Meadow, 10 acres, occupied by George Little
> Gray's Field, 15 acres, occupied by Robert Emerton
> Conduit Meadow, 6 acres, occupied by Robert Emerton
> Conduit Close, 20 acres, occupied by Elizabeth Jones.

The lawyers who drew up the conveyance included a charge on the Castle Hill which had originally been a charge on Castle House. This was: 'And save and excepted an annual quit rent or other rent of £6 1s. 4d. issuing and payable out of or in respect of the said hereditaments and premises or some part or parts thereof to Lord Middleton and his heirs for Barton's Charity in Buckingham.'

Philip Box was an active magistrate. One of his decisions, made on 18 August 1792, was to order George Bennett the younger, dealer, to pay maintenance to Mary Morris to support a bastard child, born on 18 April 1790. Like many of his predecessors at Castle House, Philip Box was deeply attached to Buckingham church, in his case the new church on Castle Hill. He presented the church with an organ, originally erected in the Western Gallery and bearing the inscription, 'Georgius King, London fecit 1801, No 24 Marsham Street, Westminster'. In his will, dated 1811, Box left £1,000, in 3 per cent consols, to the Bailiff and Burgesses of Buckingham, with the instruction that the income was to be used 'towards the support of an organist'.

When Castle House came on the market in 1798, Philip Box bought the house, but not the whole of the property. The vendors, Thomas Shillingford and his wife Susannah, had mortgaged the house to Richard Scott of Maids Moreton for £2,000. This was paid off, but the surviving abstract of title does not specify how much Philip Box paid to Thomas Shillingford over and above the sum of £2,000. The Marquis of Buckingham appears to have bought the nearby *Cross Keys Inn*. The inn was soon closed down, probably because it was a rival to the Marquis's own establishment, the *Cobham Arms*, which stood immediately east of the *Cross Keys*. It is surprising that the Marquis did not buy Castle House himself. It would have prevented any potential rival to his control of Buckingham gaining a foothold in the borough. Philip Box may, however, have been acting for the Marquis, expecting him to buy it later. Box never lived at Castle House, and continued his business from his own house in Market Hill. It would have been here that he entertained visitors like Elizabeth Fremantle, who visited 'Mrs Box' at Buckingham in October 1803 and accompanied her to Stowe.[8] Philip Box's tenants at Castle House may have included some of the Marquis's friends, and no doubt rooms at Castle House were always available if the Marquis had guests he did not care to accommodate at Stowe itself. Philip Box may even have let parts of Castle house to his own extended family, including William Box, who appears on the land tax return in 1817 as a tenant of his brother Edward Box of Carlow.

About 1803, Philip Box bought from the estate of Lord George Sackville a strip of land south west of the Brackley Road. This land had once belonging to the Castle Farm and Box may have bought it to consolidate the holding he had acquired with the Castle Hill. The major part of Lord Sackville's land was north of Castle House. This was bought by the Marquis of Buckingham and laid out as a model farm called Castle Fields Farm, occupied by his agent, George Parrott. In his will of 1811, Philip Box left the land he had purchased from Lord Sackville to his nephew, William Box. William Box's son, Philip Lord Box, held it in 1846. The Victorian houses opposite the cemetery are built on part of this land.

The Will of Philip Box of Buckingham, 1811

Philip Box died in April 1811. A portrait of him, a rather rustic-looking country gentleman, hung for many years in the church and is now in the Old Gaol Museum. His memorial declares that for more than forty years he was 'In able active service of this Borough and County'. In his will of 1811, Philip Box of Buckingham gave £1,000 and a portion of his houses and land in the town to each of the sons of his late brother, Edward Box of Bourton.

Philip Box left his house on Castle Hill, once leased by his brother, to his oldest nephew, also called Philip Box. The house was described in the will as:

> All that and those my messuage or tenement lands grounds and hereditaments situate lying and being in the Parish of Buckingham aforesaid which I bought and

purchased of and from the Trustees of the late Ralph Earl Verney deceased and also all those several messuages or tenements lately erected and built upon part of the said premises near Castle Hill Buckingham aforesaid.

The testator left Castle House to his nephew Edmund Box of Carlow in Ireland. It is described in the will as:

All that my capital messuage or tenement in Buckingham aforesaid with the yards gardens outbuildings and several closes of pasture ground adjoining and belonging which I bought and purchased of and from Mr Thomas Shillingford with all and every the rights and members and appurtenances to the same belonging save except the close of pasture ground in Buckingham aforesaid

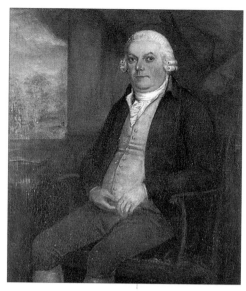

25   Philip Box, *c*.1800.

known by the name of Sawpit Close now occupied by Joseph Summerfield which I purchased subsequently to the other premises and the orchard or land called the Cherry Orchard which orchard I now occupy and which I will and desire may for ever hereafter go with and be considered as part of the premises belonging to the house and garden now in my own occupation.

Philip Box the banker left his own house in Market Hill to his nephew Thomas Box. This was probably the fine 18th-century double-fronted house demolished in the 1950s to built the Woolworth's store. It was described as:

All that my messuage or tenement wherein I now dwell and also all that messuage or tenement late in the occupation of Mrs Elizabeth Holt with the yard gardens and outbuildings thereto belonging now in my occupation which last mentioned premises were purchased of Mr John Brickwell and also all that the said close of pasture ground in Buckingham aforesaid known by the name of the Sand Pit Close or Ground now occupied by Joseph Summerfield and all that the said Cherry Orchard hereinbefore mentioned both of which I bought and purchased of and from Mr Thomas Shillingford.

Box left the remaining portion of his land to his youngest nephew, William Box of Bourton. This land was situated south of the Brackley Road and is described in the will as: 'All those my lands and premises in Buckingham aforesaid which I bought and purchased of and from Lord Sackville and others with all and singular the rights members and appurtenances thereto belonging'.

Philip Box of Hill House

Philip Box, son of Edward and Anne Box, probably worked in his uncle's bank. He married Penelope, daughter of Henry Smith, in 1796. The couple lived at Hill House, at the top of Elm Street, which his uncle had purchased from Verney's Trustees in

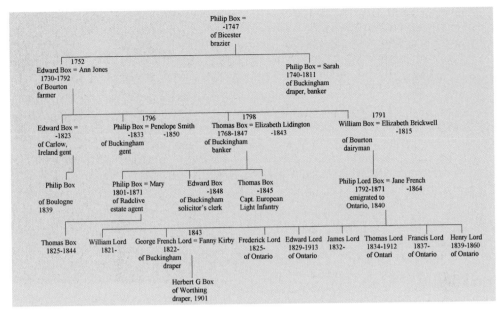

26   Box family tree.

1791. Although this property was left to Philip and Penelope in the will of Philip Box in 1811, there was a proviso to the effect that, if Philip and Penelope had no issue, then the property would descend to Box's great nephew, Philip, son of Thomas Box. As it happened, Philip and Penelope Box had no children, Philip dying in 1833 and his wife Penelope in 1850, so Hill House eventually passed to Philip Box, who was by then living in Radclive. There was a plaque on the east wall of Buckingham church to the memory of Philip Box (of this town), who died 22 August 1833 aged 76; and of Mrs Mary Clarke (widow), who died March 1820, aged 90'.

Edward Box of Carlow

The second son of Edward and Anne Box of Bourton was also called Edward. He seems to have worked for his uncle and may have represented Box's bank in Ireland, where the bank's main customer, the Marquis of Buckingham, was Lord Lieutenant from 1782-3 and 1787-9. Edward Box had married Sarah Curly and was living in the town of Carlow, in Ireland, when Philip Box the banker made his will in 1811. He left Castle House to his nephew Edward Box of Carlow on the understanding that, if he and his wife had no children, then the property would ultimately descend to Box's great nephew, Philip Box, son of Thomas Box. In the event, Edward Box of Carlow did have a son, Philip, who should have inherited Castle House on his parents' deaths.

Edward Box of Carlow was still acting as agent to the Marquis of Buckingham in 1813 when he was dealing with the Grenvilles' tenants in West Leath.[11] He was also managing his own property in Buckingham. In 1817 he was renting an un-named but significant property in the Borough of Buckingham to his brother, William Box, who paid £3 17s. 9d. land tax for it. This was in all probability Castle House. When Edward Box of Carlow made his will in 1823, however, he described his estate in

Buckingham as 'houses and land in the Town of Buckingham in England heretofore let to the Duke of Buckingham'. The freehold of Castle House should have passed to Edward Box's widow and then to his son Philip, who was under 21 in 1823.

Edward Box of Carlow also had two daughters, Elizabeth Anne and Sarah Jane, each of whom were left £1,500. It is not clear whether these children ever received their inheritances, for payment of Edward Box's legacies depended on his trustees being able to recover 'my part or proportion of the bond debts due by the said Duke [of Buckingham] being one fourth part of the same amounting to the sum of nine hundred and twenty four pounds British money'. Edward Box left the remainder of his 'property and effects not hereby specifically bequeathed but chargeable as aforesaid to my said trustees as aforesaid and the survivor of them in trust for the use and benefit of my nephews Thomas and Edward Box sons of my brother Thomas Box equally between them share and share alike'. Perhaps Edward Box of Carlow was still involved in his brother Thomas Box's Buckingham Old Bank and was caught up in the collapse of the bank in 1824? His exact date of death is not known but his will was proved in London in September 1825.

Thomas Box of Maids Moreton

Edward Box of Bourton's third son, Thomas Box, was baptised at Buckingham in 1768. He married Elizabeth Lidington at Buckingham in 1798. The couple had a son, Philip Box, born in 1801, and two younger sons, Thomas and Edward. Thomas Box became a Burgess of Buckingham on 13 May 1807, and was Bailiff in 1809 and 1817. In his will of 1811, Philip Box the banker left his own dwelling house in Market Hill to his nephew Thomas Box. He also left several closes of meadow and pasture in the Prebend End of Buckingham, which he had purchased from Henry Flowers, to Thomas's son Philip, the land to be held by his trustees during the boy's minority and the income from it to be used to pay for his education. This Philip Box, born in 1801, matriculated at Brasenose College, Oxford in October 1818, aged 17. There were two younger sons, Thomas and Edward. Thomas Box became a soldier with the East India Company; Edward Box became a clerk with the Buckingham solicitors, Hearn & Nelson. In 1841 he was living with his father, Thomas Box, at Maids Moreton. He gave his age as 25 and his occupation as 'legal profession'.

Thomas Box continued his uncle's bank as the 'Buckingham Old Bank'. His partners in the bank were Edward Oakley Gray, solicitor, who lived at Maids Moreton, and George Parrott, who occupied Castle Fields Farm, west of the avenue

27 Buckingham Old Bank note, 1815, signed by Thomas Box.

to Stowe. Thomas Box's signature appears on a bank note issued by Messrs Box, Gray & Parrott, Buckingham in 1815.[9] George Parrott left the partnership with Thomas Box in 1821 and continued on his own as G. Parrott & Co. Parrott's bank later amalgamated with Bartlett & Co. to become Bartlett, Parrott & Co., and later Bartlett, Parrott & Hearn. Parrott was wise to leave Box's bank, as in April 1824 Thomas Box of Buckingham, banker, was declared bankrupt. The bankruptcy proceedings continued until 1828. The bankruptcy trustees sold most of Thomas Box's Buckingham property, including the Sand Pit Closes behind his house in Market Hill, which were purchased by his former partner, George Parrott, then living at Castle Fields Farm. Thomas Box himself retired to Maids Moreton where he rented a house from Richard Scott. His wife Elizabeth died there in 1843, aged 68. Thomas Box himself died in 1847 and was buried at Maids Moreton. Their eldest son, Philip Box, became an auctioneer in Buckingham. He later lived at Radclive, where he died in 1871. Their second son, Thomas Box, was a Captain in the European Light Infantry and died of wounds received at Ferozeshah, one of the battles of the First Sikh War, in 1845. Their third son, Edward Box, became a solicitor's clerk, working for Messrs Hearn & Nelson in Buckingham. He died in 1848 at the age of 35 and was buried at Buckingham.

William Box of Bourton

Edward Box of Bourton's fourth son, William Box, took over the lease of Pound Farm, Bourton on his father's death in 1792. He paid £27 7s. 9d. land tax on his Bourton property in 1795. According to the Posse Comitatus, compiled in 1798, he had four horses, two wagons and two carts there. William Box had married Elizabeth Brickwell at Buckingham in 1791. The couple had several children, all baptised at the Independent Meeting House in Well Street. The eldest of these was Philip Lord Box, baptised in 1792. In his will of 1811, Philip Box the banker left to his nephew William several closes of land between the Brackley Road and the river which he had purchased from Lord Sackville.

William Box of Bourton's wife, Elizabeth, died in 1815, aged 50. In 1816 William Box, widower, married Elizabeth Stokes, spinster, and moved into Buckingham, leaving his son Philip Lord Box in charge of the farm at Bourton. William and his new wife Elizabeth may have lived at Castle House, which was then owned by William's brother, Edward Box, of Carlow in Ireland. According to the land tax returns of 1817, he paid £3 17s. 9d. tax on a property owned by Edward Box. This would be logical as William Box would be receiving income from the nearby land on the Brackley Road, on which £4 2s. 6½d. tax was paid, occupied by a tenant named Rogers. There may have been a house on this land for the 1841 census lists a 'Box's Farm', occupied by ... Holt and situated near George Parrott's Castle Fields Farm. On the 1846 Tithe Map, the land on the Brackley Road is owned by William Box's son, Philip Lord Box, and occupied by John Sheppard.

The Sale of Castle House

In 1884 the then owner of Castle House, Henry Hearn, solicitor of Buckingham, gave a guided tour of his house and told his guests that 'about the year 1835, the property was purchased by Mr Thomas Hearn from Mr Philip Box, the representative of the Irish branch of the family'. A different account of the purchase is given in 'Notes on the Hearn Family of Buckingham', compiled about 1940 by Sir Gordon Hearn and now in the possession of James Hearn of Greenwich. According to this source, 'Castle House in West Street or Fowler Street, Buckingham was purchased by Thomas Hearn, solicitor, of Buckingham, on 18 Nov. 1837 from Philip Lord Box of Radclive, late of Clapham Road, Surrey.' A conveyance of the same date is referred to in the sale particulars drawn up in July 1903, when the executors of Henry Hearn put Castle House up for auction. The Hearn family information about the sale must be garbled, for Philip Lord Box and Philip Box of Radclive were two very different individuals, and the most likely person to have lived in Clapham was Philip, son of Edward Box of Carlow. The Hearn family information may in fact be based upon a cursory reading of more than one conveyance, for the 1903 sale particulars recite another deed of 21 June 1838 by which land to the rear of Castle House was conveyed to Thomas Hearn.

There was clearly some dispute over title to the property at the time. In 1839 Thomas Hearn, the purchaser of Castle House, persuaded Penelope Box, widow of the Philip Box who had died in 1833, to make a written declaration as to the relationship of her late husband, with Philip Box the banker and other members of the Box family still living. The document reads as follows:

> I Penelope Box of Buckingham in the County of Bucks widow do solemnly and sincerely declare that I am now of eighty three years or thereabouts and that I am the widow of Philip Box late of Buckingham aforesaid gentleman deceased who died without issue in the month of August in the year 1833 and was buried at Buckingham aforesaid
>
> That I knew and was well acquainted with Philip Box formerly of Buckingham aforesaid Esq deceased who died in the month of April in the year 1811 and was likewise buried at Buckingham aforesaid
>
> That the last named Philip Box died without issue
>
> That Edward Box formerly of Bicester but afterwards of Bourton in the parish of Buckingham aforesaid was the only brother of the said last named Philip Box and my said late husband the first named Philip Box was the oldest son of the said Edward Box as I have always understood and verily believe
>
> That Edward Box late of Carlow in Ireland deceased was the brother of the first named Philip Box (my late husband)
>
> That no older brother of the last named Edward Box survived the said first named Philip Box or died in his lifetime leaving issue
>
> That the said last named Edward Box died in the year 1823 leaving an only son Philip Box now or late resident at Boulogne sur Mer in the Kingdom of France as I have always understood and verily believe.[10]

Philip, son of Edward Box of Carlow

Philip Box, son of Edward Box of Carlow, should have inherited Castle House on the death of his father in 1823. In 1825 Philip married Ann Coughlan of Rathtoe. The Buckingham voters list of 1833 includes a Philip Box of 10 Dorset Place, Clapham, whose tenants in Buckingham (probably at Castle House) were Mrs Seeley and others (John Seeley, stationer, had been Philip Box's executor in 1811). According to Penelope Box, however, by 1839 Philip Box, the son of Edward Box of Carlow, was living in Boulogne, a well-known refuge for bankrupt English gentlemen. In 1841 a Philip Box, aged 25, describing himself as a teacher, was living at Furnivals

Inn, London. With him were his wife, Ann, and their children, Edward, Philip, Ann and Mary, all of whom were born in Ireland. By 1851 a Philip Box, aged 45, born in Carlow, Ireland, was lodging in Old Compton Street, Westminster describing himself as a Professor of Languages. By 1861 the same Philip Box and his wife Ann were living at 28 George Street, Marylebone. His occupation was given as 'teacher of the English language'. If this Philip Box was in fact the son of Edward Box of Carlow, he either did not receive the purchase money for Castle House in 1837, or he ran through it remarkably quickly.

Philip Lord Box

Philip Lord Box, son of William Box of Bourton, was born in 1792. In 1816 he married Jane, daughter of George French of Buckingham, and took over the tenancy of the family farm in Bourton. He paid a very substantial £28 7s. 11d. land tax on his Bourton property in 1817. He also inherited land on the Brackley Road from his father, William Box, and was still holding it in 1846 when the Tithe Map was drawn up. He certainly did not inherit Castle House, however. Philip Lord Box and Jane had several children baptised at Buckingham from 1821-34, including William, George, Frederick, Edward, Philip, James and Thomas, all of whom were given the middle name of Lord. Throughout this period the family lived at Bourton, not at Radclive. Philip Lord Box left Buckingham about 1837, and his two youngest children, Francis and Henry, were born in Bedford. The whole family emigrated to Canada in 1840. Philip Lord Box would hardly have undertaken the risk and hardship of emigration if he had recently received the purchase money for Castle House. Philip Lord Box died in Oxford County, Ontario in 1871. Several of his sons became well-to-do farmers in Ontario.

Philip Box of Radclive

Under the terms of the 1811 will of Philip Box the banker, if Philip and Penelope Box of Hill House had no children, then Hill House was to descend to his great nephew Philip Box, son of his nephew Thomas Box. In the event this Philip Box, who lived at Radclive from 1828 until 1871, did inherit Hill House on the death of Penelope Box in 1850. Another provision of the 1811 will was that if Edward Box of Carlow were to have no children then Castle House was also to descend to the banker's great nephew Philip Box. In fact, Edward Box of Carlow had a son, also called Philip Box, so Thomas's son, Philip, was unlikely to inherit Castle House.

Philip, son of Thomas Box, was born in 1801. As early as 1821 the young Philip Box, recently a student at Brasenose College, Oxford and no doubt heavily in debt, used his expectation of inheriting Hill House, on the deaths of Philip and Penelope Box, as security for a loan from Philip and Thomas Bartlett of Buckingham, woolstaplers. His father, Thomas Box, went bankrupt in 1824, so the young man could not ask for help from that quarter. In 1828, describing himself as a gentleman and living at Radclive, Philip Box used the security of Hill House to raise a further loan of £500 from a London jeweller called William Rose.

Philip Box of Radclive was certainly in need of cash and would have been only too happy to sell property to Thomas Hearn in 1837. There seems no way, however, that he could have established a claim to Castle House and conveyed it to Thomas Hearn whilst his cousin Philip, son of Edward Box of Carlow, was still alive. Philip

Box of Radclive could, however, have acted as an agent for the wider Box family in facilitating the sale to Thomas Hearn. Alternatively, he could have bought out his Irish cousin, Philip Box, and sold on to Thomas Hearn at a profit. He could also have helped his other cousin, Philip Lord Box, to sell some land near Castle House to Thomas Hearn in 1838. He was in an ideal position to make these arrangements as his younger brother, Edward Box, was a clerk in Thomas Hearn's legal practice.

Philip Box of Radclive's financial position does seem to have improved at this time. In 1841 he was living next door to the Rectory at Radclive, with his wife Mary, aged 30, and his son Thomas, aged 15. He described himself on the census as an auctioneer, and the family had one live-in servant. His son Thomas Box died in 1844, aged 19, and was buried at Radclive. Philip Box of Radclive was Mayor of Buckingham in 1852. He stood as a parliamentary candidate for Buckingham in the election of 1857, but received only 82 votes. He died at Radclive in 1871 aged 69. His widow, Mary Box, was still living there in 1891 aged 87. It could well be that Philip Box of Radclive, who had no real claim to Castle House, nevertheless profited from its sale by Philip Box of Boulogne in 1837, and from the sale of the nearby land by Philip Lord Box in 1838.

Chapter Eight

THE HEARNS:
THE LAW AND THE PROFITS

THOMAS HEARN, a yeoman farmer from Grendon Underwood, had two sons, William (1746-1836), who continued to farm the family land there, and Thomas (1749-1827), who set up as an attorney in Buckingham in 1775. The young attorney prospered and by 1784 he owned a substantial house in West Street, occupied farmland at Chackmore, and called himself a gentleman.

Thomas Hearn, Attorney

In 1784 Thomas Hearn insured his premises with the Sun Insurance Company:

	£
Thomas Hearn of the Town of Buckingham gent	
On his now dwelling house offices and barn all	
adjoining situate as aforesaid brick and tiled	500
Household goods therein only	200
Printed books therein only	50
Wearing apparel	50
Utensils and stock viz:	
In his two barns adjoining at Chackmore in Bucks thatched	60
In his barn only separate thatched	40
	900[1]

It may have been the Hearn family's connections with the Verneys of Claydon which took Thomas Hearn to Buckingham. Hearn was a trustee for the 1777 rebuilding of Buckingham church on Castle Hill, then owned by Earl Verney. He acted for the Verneys in the sale of their estates in Bourton and Lenborough in 1792, and was himself tenant of one of the larger Lenborough farms in 1795. Thomas Hearn was also party to an agreement for the sale of the Castle Hill, from Verney's trustees to Philip Box, in May 1791.[2] In 1797 Thomas Hearn purchased farmland in Singleborough from Mary Verney, Baroness Fermanagh. He and his nephew, Thomas Hearn, were later to become parliamentary agents for the Verney family, and were prominent in the elections for the Buckingham seats in the 19th century.[3] Thomas Hearn also had a farm at Hardwick, near Aylesbury, which he held by lease from New College, Oxford.

Thomas Hearn married Susannah Wells, daughter of the Rev. Joseph Wells of Ellesborough near Wendover. According to their marriage settlement, his wife Susannah would be entitled to an estate in Wendover, subject to a mortgage for £1,000 given by Thomas Hearn to discharge a debt previously incurred by the Rev. Wells. Thomas and Susannah Hearn had no children. For this reason, Hearn invited his nephew, Thomas Hearn (1782-1865), son of his brother William Hearn, to join him in Buckingham.

The Will of Thomas Hearn

Thomas Hearn's original house, later numbered 27 West Street, was a timber-framed three-bay house, two storeys high, with dormer windows to the attics. It was separated from the street by iron railings and had stone steps up to the central front door. On its west side (now numbered 26 West Street) was an early 18th-century brick-built extension with an archway (now blocked by a bay window) giving access to the coachhouse and stables. We get some impression of Thomas Hearn's household from his will, made 7 September 1823. Although he left most of his property to his wife, Susannah, during her life, he stipulated that his nephew and business partner, Thomas Hearn, would have immediate access to his own and his clerk's office in his dwelling house in Buckingham, with access at all reasonable times through the passage leading to these offices. He mentioned other rooms in the house, leaving his wife Susannah the furniture in the dining room and drawing room, the chintz bedroom, his usual sleeping room and his dressing room adjoining. His nephew Thomas Hearn, was to have all the desks, tables, drawers, books, papers and other effects in his own and his clerk's office, along with his other books, except those formerly belonging to his wife, and any more which she might select for her own reading. He also gave his wife his little four-wheeled open carriage, with the horses, harness and furniture.

Thomas Hearn junior

Thomas Hearn's solicitor's practice was continued by his nephew, Thomas Hearn, son of his brother William Hearn of Grendon Underwood. Thomas Hearn junior first appeared in Buckingham society when commissioned as a Lieutenant in the Bucks Militia, in 1808, and later as a Captain, in 1809. Thomas Hearn junior was

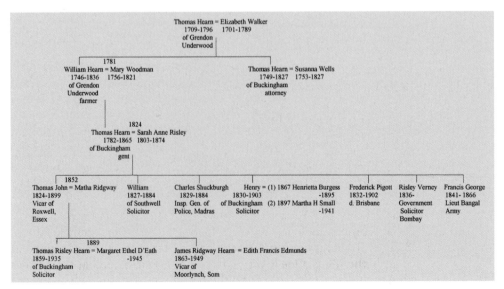

28　Hearn family tree.

29   Thomas Hearn, *c*.1860.

30   Sarah Anne Hearn, *c*.1860.

the highest bidder at £6,800 for the lease of Maids Moreton Manor House in 1816.[4] This house and about 250 acres of land belonged to All Souls College, Oxford, and had been occupied by Edward Oakley Gray, the Buckingham solicitor and partner in Box's bank, who died in that year. Thomas Hearn does not appear to have lived at Maids Moreton. According to George Lipscomb, the house was sub-let to Francis Godolphin Osborne, brother of the Duke of Leeds. In 1831 Thomas Hearn paid land tax of £15 10s. 3½d. on his farmland at Maids Moreton, which was occupied by George Markam and George Butcher. Hearn renewed the lease from All Souls College in 1829 and in 1836, but in 1840 he sold the remainder of his lease to the Duke of Buckingham for £11,000.[5] The Manor House was rebuilt around 1883 and is currently used as an old people's home.

In 1824 Thomas Hearn married Sarah Ann Risley, daughter of the Rev. John Risley of Tingewick. Risley's father, also named John Risley, had been presented to the Rectory of Tingewick by the Warden and Scholars of New College, Oxford in 1759, and held it for 60 years. Thomas and Sarah Hearn had 11 children, the eldest of whom, the Rev. Thomas John Hearn, was born in 1824 and became a fellow of New College, Oxford. He was Rector of Roxwell, in Essex, for 48 years.

Another son of Thomas and Sarah Ann Hearn, Charles Shuckburgh Hearn, was born in 1829. This young man wrote regularly to his mother when a pupil at Winchester College in the 1840s. One letter in particular is worth quoting as it throws light on the young man's choice of career and the friendly relationship which existed between the Hearns and the Box family, their predecessors at Castle House:

31   The Rev. Thomas John Hearn and family, *c*.1890.

Winchester, 6 March 1846

It seems to have been a most splendid battle in India. I saw the name of Capt. T. Box among the killed and concluded that it was Edward Box's brother. It is certainly very unfortunate that after doing so well, and being on the eve of returning home, he should be killed in his last battle, but he died a soldier's death and his regiment seems to have distinguished itself greatly. I suppose cadetships will be rather more plentiful now. I should still like very well to get one as I really do not quite see my way as to what I am to do.

The 'Captain T. Box' referred to in the letter is in fact Thomas, son of Thomas Box, the Buckingham banker who had gone bankrupt in 1824. Thomas's elder brother Philip was an auctioneer in Buckingham and another brother, Edward, also referred to in the letter, was a clerk working for Charles Shuckburgh Hearn's father, Thomas Hearn. Charles did in fact join the army and saw service in the Crimean War and the Indian Mutiny. He became Inspector General of Police, Madras, in 1867. He retired to England in 1881 and died in Hove in 1884. Another son of Thomas and Sarah Anne Hearn, Henry Hearn, was born in 1830 and became a partner in his father's legal firm in Buckingham in 1852.

Thomas Hearn made alterations to his house and offices, now numbered 26-7 West Street. No. 27 was let to Sarah Brett and later to Dr Robert De'ath, whose unfortunate name did not prevent him becoming one of the leading physicians in the neighbourhood. The coach entrance through No. 26 was blocked and replaced by an office with a large bay window. It is unlikely that these alterations were carried out before Thomas Hearn's purchase of Castle House in 1837. The carriage entrance was vital to the convenient use of 27 West Street as a genteel family home.

Thomas Hearn extended his business interests in Buckingham, taking into partnership George Nelson, who was for many years Town Clerk to the Borough of Buckingham. Their firm was known as Hearn & Nelson. Thomas Hearn also became a partner in the local bank, now styled Bartlett, Parrot & Hearn. This was merged into the Bucks and Oxon Union Bank in 1853. Thomas Hearn also acted as agent to the Verneys in their contests with the Grenvilles of Stowe for the two seats in Parliament which Buckingham enjoyed until the second Reform Act. In 1832 he issued a 'Friendly address to the electors of Buckingham and its boundary parishes' in his own name.[6] He even gave his son Risley Hearn, born in 1836, the middle name of Verney. Thomas Hearn was elected to the new Buckingham Borough Council following the Municipal Corporations Act, and was Mayor of Buckingham in 1837.

32   Charles Shuckburgh Hearn (1829-84).

Thomas Hearn's Purchase of Castle House

It was natural that Thomas Hearn should seek to express his elevated position in Buckingham society in the choice of a permanent family home. Thus it was that he managed to buy Castle House from the Box family in 1837. Until a copy or abstract of the conveyance is located, we cannot be sure how he came to buy the house, or

33   Castle House, 1845.

whether the then representatives of the
Box family really had the right to sell
it. Nonetheless, Thomas Hearn enjoyed
his new house at Buckingham for nearly
forty years. The house he purchased
was quadrangular but, on the advice
of the young George Gilbert Scott, he
demolished the north range and opened
the remainder up to the garden.

In January 1845 Queen Victoria passed
through Buckingham on her way to Stowe,
where she spent several days as the guest of
the Duke of Buckingham. It is said that his
lavish hospitality hastened his bankruptcy
in 1848. Amongst the newspaper reporters
who followed the royal progress was a
correspondent of the *Illustrated London
News*. He was evidently told of an earlier
royal visit, for he included in his report

34   Thomas Hearn, *c*.1865.

a drawing of a 'house at Buckingham where Charles I lodged'.[7] The building is
unmistakably the west wing of Castle House, although it is not called by this name
in the article. There is no suggestion that Queen Victoria stopped at Castle House
as her coach passed by, but it is highly likely that Thomas Hearn hoped to gain
some reflected glory by being associated with a royal visit. The drawing shows the
stone mullioned windows of the Great Parlour and the two-storey bay window on
the north wall. The bay window is much as it is today, with what appears to be the
Lambert datestone in its present position between the two windows. This suggests
that the architect Swinfen Harris, who worked on this part of the house in 1881,
made only modest alterations.

In 1851 Thomas Hearn and his family were living at Castle House with a governess
and five servants. As his children gradually left home and married, the number of
servants was reduced to three. The east wing, with its separate garden, was let to
Edward Bond, veterinary surgeon, and Bond was still living there in 1871, with his
wife Charlotte and son William, who was also training to be a veterinary surgeon.
After Edward Bond's death, his business was continued by his wife Charlotte, but
by 1891 the east wing was occupied by Charles Marsh, an insurance agent.

The Death of Thomas Hearn

Thomas Hearn of Buckingham, gentleman, made his will on 4 May 1857:

> I hereby direct or authorize the trustees or trustee of this my will at any time
> after my decease to sell the messuage or tenement and premises situate in West
> Street in the Town of Buckingham now in the occupation of Mrs Sarah Brett
> and also the professional offices thereto adjoining as now occupied by myself and
> professional co-partners with the appurtenances to the same respectively belonging
> to my said son Henry Hearn if he shall be desirous of purchasing the same.

According to this will, Thomas Hearn had paid a £200 deposit on a property
which had been lot 11 in the recent sale of the Duke of Buckingham's estate. This

may well have been 25 West Street. This property, however, is shown on the plan prepared for the 1894 sale of a further part of the late Duke's estate as still belonging to Lady Kinloss. Perhaps Thomas Hearn bought only part of this property. This would explain why the new extension to the solicitor's offices, built by his son Henry Hearn, does not extend to the whole of 25 West Street.

Thomas Hearn died on 22 August 1865 and was buried in the old churchyard, Buckingham. A pulpit in the church of St Peter and Paul was given in his memory. His widow, Sarah Anne Hearn, died at Castle House on 23 March 1874 and was also buried in the old churchyard. In her will, she divided amongst her many children a bewildering array of jewellery, furniture and personal effects, leaving the remainder to her son Henry Hearn, 'in just acknowledgement of his liberal and ready help towards the expense of keeping up my present establishment'. There is a stained glass window in the church of St Peter and Paul to the memory of Sarah Ann Hearn. Following her death, Castle House was valued by estate agents Jonas Paxton of Bicester and George Bennett & Son of Buckingham. In the event Castle House was not sold, and in 1875 Henry Hearn came to an agreement with his brothers, Thomas John Hearn, Charles Shuckburgh Hearn and Risley Verney Hearn, by which he was able to maintain the house. The arrangement was modified by a further agreement between the brothers in 1884.[8]

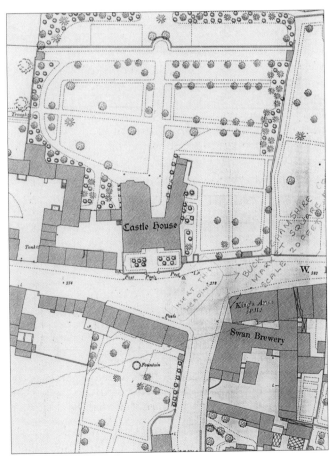

35   Castle House, from an Ordnance Survey map of Buckingham drawn up in 1880.

Henry Hearn of Castle House

Henry Hearn was born in 1830 and became a partner with his father, Thomas Hearn, and George Nelson in 1852. The firm was then called Hearn, Nelson & Hearn. After the death of George Nelson in 1876, George Frederick Wellington Langdon joined the partnership, which was known as Nelson, Hearn & Langdon and later as Hearn & Langdon. When Henry Hearn's nephew, Thomas Risley Hearn, replaced Langdon, the name was changed again to Hearn & Hearn. Henry Hearn was a member of the Town Council and was Mayor in 1871. He succeeded his partner George Nelson as Town Clerk, and was also Clerk to the Rural District Council, the Board of Guardians and the Burial Board. He was also a director of the Bucks & Oxon Union Bank. He was a churchwarden for 30 years and a member of the Buckingham Charity Trustees. He was agent to Sir Harry Verney in successive elections for the Member of Parliament for Buckingham. Henry Hearn made considerable alterations to his offices in West Street. The premises immediately to the west of the office with the bay window was rebuilt in brick with stone dressings, and a purpose-built muniment room was added to the rear.

In 1881 Henry Hearn employed the architect Edward Swinfen Harris, of Stony Stratford, to restore the west wing of Castle House. The two gothic windows in the west wall were re-glazed and the bay window in the north wall was restored. Swinfen Harris may well have embellished the fireplace in the Great Parlour which features the Lambert initials. According to Thomas Silvester, writing about 1840, this 'curious chimney piece of carved oak' was then in one of the bedrooms.[9] In

August 1884 members of the Bucks Archaeological Society, on an excursion to Buckingham and Stowe, were given an outline of the history of Buckingham, its church, the Latin School and Castle House, by the vicar, the Rev. F.G. Kiddle. He compared the warm reception given by Lady Richardson to Charles I on his visiting Castle House in 1644 to that the members could expect that day from the present owner, Mr Henry Hearn. On their reaching the house, they were indeed received by Henry Hearn, who read his own paper on the history of the house, beginning with the will of John Barton in 1431. He described the major alterations made by Matthias Rogers in 1708, and his own more modest changes in 1881.[10]

Henry Hearn had married Henrietta Burgess in London in 1867. There were no children and Henrietta Hearn died in 1895. Henry Hearn didn't remain a widower for long. In 1897 he married Martha Henrietta Small, the daughter of

IN THE BOROUGH OF BUCKINGHAM.

PARTICULARS, PLAN, VIEWS AND CONDITIONS OF SALE
OF AN
EXCEEDINGLY INTERESTING AND ATTRACTIVE
Freehold Residential Property
KNOWN AS
"The Castle House Estate,"

Situate on the outskirts of the Town and occupying an advantageous and commanding position. The Station on the Bletchley and Banbury branch of the London and North Western Railway is about 10 minutes' walk, whence London may be reached in 1¾ hours (facilitated on certain trains by "through" carriages), and Finmere Station on the Great Central line is within five miles of the property.

THE ESTATE

COMPRISES AN EXCEEDINGLY COMFORTABLE
FAMILY RESIDENCE

Built of Brick with Freestone Dressings and Tiled Roof, representing a very fine specimen of the late Tudor style of architecture. The house is also of exceptional interest on account of its historical associations, it having been visited by Royalty on different occasions, and Councils of War held within its walls. The Residence contains:—Entrance Hall, 3 handsome Reception Rooms (the Dining Room with its old Oak fitments being especially fine), 11 good Bed and Dressing Rooms, 6 Servants' Attic Rooms, and commodious Domestic Offices and Cellarage. There is a delightful old-world Garden and Wilderness Orchard, Fruit and Vegetable Garden with 3 Greenhouses, Stabling Accommodation for 6 Horses, double Coachhouse and Harness Room. The property also comprises 5 Valuable Enclosures of Building or

ACCOMMODATION PASTURE LAND
FOUR SMALL HOUSES

Forming Nos. 9, 10, 11 and 12, West Street) with Gardens and Outbuildings, a newly-erected COTTAGE with GARDEN, the whole extending over an area of upwards of
25 ACRES.
The Property is handsomely timbered, and the timber will be included in the Sale.

Messrs. WALTON AND LEE
IN CONJUNCTION WITH
Messrs. **GEORGE BENNETT & SONS**

Have received instructions from T. R. HEARN, Esq., Trustee for Sale under the Will of the late HENRY HEARN, Esq., to offer the above for Sale by Auction, at the

WHITE HART HOTEL, BUCKINGHAM
On **WEDNESDAY, the 15th day of JULY, 1903,**

At 2 for 3 o'clock precisely, first as a whole, and if not sold in that manner then in two lots (unless previously disposed of by private treaty).

Copies of these Particulars may be obtained of Messrs. HEARN & HEARN, Solicitors, Buckingham; Messrs. GEORGE BENNETT & SONS, Estate Agents and Auctioneers, Buckingham; and of Messrs. WALTON & LEE, Auctioneers and Surveyors, 10, Mount Street, Grosvenor Square, London, W.

G. F. MARSH, PRINTER, 10, MARKET SQUARE, BUCKINGHAM.

36   Castle House sale catalogue, 1903.

the late Edward F. Small and niece of a rival Buckingham solicitor, Henry Small, of Steeple Claydon. When Henry Hearn himself died on 8 April 1903; his second wife, Martha Henrietta, did not stay on at Castle House, but moved to Overn Hill, Buckingham, the home of her brother Edward Henry Small, solicitor. She died there on 22 September 1941.

The Sale of Castle House

Castle House was put up for auction at the *White Hart Hotel*, Buckingham on 15 July 1903. It was described as:

> An exceedingly comfortable family residence, built of brick with freestone dressings and tiled roof, representing a very fine specimen of the late Tudor style of architecture. The house is also of exceptional interest on account of its historical associations, it having been visited by royalty on different occasions, and councils of war held within its walls. The residence contains: entrance hall, 3 handsome reception rooms (the dining room with its old oak fitments being especially fine), 11 good bed and dressing rooms, 6 servants attic rooms, and commodious domestic offices and cellarage. There is a delightful old-world garden and wilderness orchard, fruit and vegetable garden with 3 greenhouses, stabling accommodation for 6 horses, double coach house and harness room. The property also comprises 5 valuable enclosures of building or accommodation pasture land, four small houses (forming nos 9, 10, 11 and 12 West Street) with gardens and outbuildings, a newly erected cottage and garden, the whole extending over an area of upwards of 25 acres.

The east wing of Castle House was occupied by Charles Marsh, at a rent of £12 per year. It was described as:

> A desirable residence, known as No. 9 West Street, situated immediately to the east of Castle House and originally a wing thereof ... The house contains entrance lobby, 2 sitting rooms, kitchen, scullery with sink and copper, to which both the town and conduit water is laid on; tool house and coal house. On the first floor are 3 bedrooms and a box room. On the second floor two attics and in the basement are 3 cellars.[11]

Castle House and 25 acres of land was purchased in 1904 by Herbert Edward Bull, a director of the Aylesbury Brewery Company, then living at the Brewery House, 4 Castle Street, Buckingham.

Although Castle House was sold, Henry Hearn's business at 26 West Street was carried on by his nephew Thomas Risley Hearn. Born in 1859, Thomas Risley Hearn was the son of the Rev. Thomas John Hearn, Rector of Roxwell, Essex, and later of Wootton, near Woodstock. In 1889 Thomas Risley Hearn married Margaret, the daughter of Robert De'Ath, surgeon, who occupied the Hearn's old house at 27 West Street. When De'Ath's son George built Hamilton House in 1892, 27 West Street was let to William Hartland, an ironmonger. The premises were later to be taken over by Reginald Culson, baker. When Thomas Risley Hearn took over the solicitor's practice in 1903, he was living at Chandos Lodge, Chandos Road, but he later moved to a new house, Roxwell House, Moreton Road. Thomas Risley Hearn had already taken over the position of Town Clerk in 1888, a position he held until 1913. He was also Clerk to the Board of Guardians, 1888-1930, and Clerk to the Rural

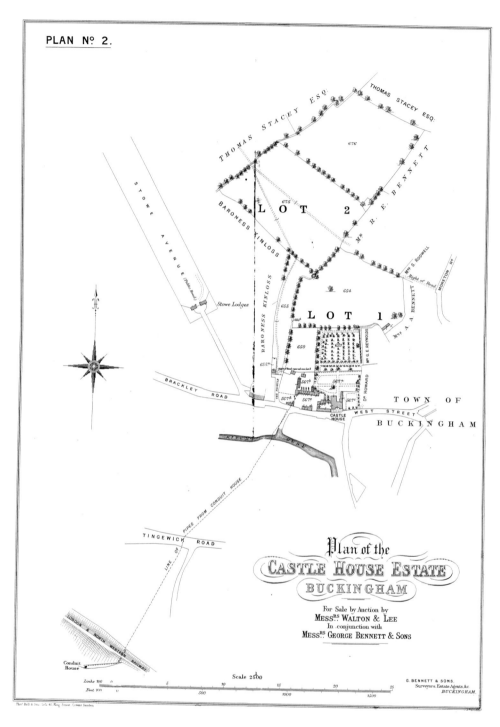

37   Castle House sale catalogue plan, 1903.

38   Castle House sale of
furniture, 1903.

Castle House, Buckingham,

Within 10 minutes' walk of Buckingham Station, L. & N.W. Ry., and
4½ miles from Finmere Station. G.C.R.

CATALOGUE OF SALE
OF THE

Valuable Antique & Modern
HOUSEHOLD FURNITURE,

Forming the Contents of the above Residence, the Estate having been sold.

GEORGE BENNETT & SONS

Are favoured with instructions from T. R. Hearn, Esq., Executor of the Will
of the late Henry Hearn, Esq., TO SELL BY AUCTION on the Premises,

On TUESDAY, DECEMBER 1st, 1903,
And two following days,

Commencing at 10-30 each day for 11 o'clock punctually,

The APPOINTMENTS of 4 RECEPTION ROOMS,

Included in which are Axminster and Brussels Carpets, Oriental Rugs,
Fenders and Nursery Guards, Rosewood Davenports, Mahogany and Rose-
wood Whatnots, Mahogany Bureau, Spring and Hair-stuffed Couches and
Easy Chairs, Kneehole Library Tables,

A JACOBEAN BUFFET SIDEBOARD,

Mahogany Dining Table, Suites in leather, Walnut and Mahogany Sideboards,
In-laid Mahogany, Carved Oak, Walnut Sutherland and other Tables, Rose-
wood and Mahogany Occasional Chairs Chippendale, Mahogany and open
Bookcases, Oak Hall Tables,

Two finely Carved Antique Scroll-back Chairs,

A PAIR OF CHIPPENDALE STOOLS, CHAMBER ORGAN WITH 4 STOPS,

Buhl and Grandfather's Clocks, an Orrery, two well-modelled Marble Statu-
ettes, Oil Paintings attributed to Holbein, Both and in part to D. Teniers,
Junr., Engravings and Prints ;

Upwards of 1,000 Volumes of Books,

300 Ounces of Silver, Sheffield Plate, English and Oriental China,

The Contents of the Bed and Dressing Rooms,

Consisting of Brass French and Arabian Bedsteads, Feather Beds, Wool and
Hair Mattresses, Blankets, Marble-top Washstands, In-laid and Spanish
Mahogany chests of Drawers, Cheval Glasses, Wardrobes in Mahogany and
Walnut, Linen Cupboards, Tapestry, Chenille, Damask and Dimity Curtains ;
also

Valuable Antique Dinner Service of 160 Pieces,

Spode Dessert Service, Cut-glass, Antique Chamber Candlesticks,
Kitchen Requisites ;

A well-built VICTORIA and an excellent BROUGHAM,

2 Sets of Black and Silver-plated Harness, Chaff-cutter, and many other
useful items.

On View the day prior to the Sale from 9 to 4, and on the
mornings of Sale up to 11 o'clock only.

Catalogues may be obtained of the Auctioneers, Buckingham.

39   Thomas Risley Hearn
and his wife Margaret, *c.*1920.

District Council. Thomas Risley Hearn continued the business as Hearn & Hearn,
26 West Street, until his own death at Roxwell House on 8 March 1935.

The good will of Hearn & Hearn was sold to Martin Fredrick Athay, whose firm
was known as Hearn & Athay. Athay rented the east wing of Castle House, which
he called The Old Cottage. He and his wife Mary had at least two children at The
Old Cottage, both delivered by Dr John Bostock, whose surgery was immediately
opposite. Martin Athay later took into partnership George Lorimer. The firm is
now known as Lorimers, and still has offices at 26 West Street in 2006.

Chapter Nine

THE BULLS:
BEER AND CHAMPAGNE

The Bull family came to Buckinghamshire in 1838, when the Rev. Henry Bull (1797-1888) was presented to the Rectory of Lathbury by the Dean and Canons of Christ Church, Oxford. Lathbury was a small parish to the north of Newport Pagnell, with a population of about 150 people, but the ample Rectory enabled the Rev. Bull and his wife Frances to entertain the best families in the district. Their son, Henry Edward, born in 1843, was educated at Westminster and Christ Church and played cricket for the University, Buckinghamshire and the MCC. In 1867 Henry Edward Bull married Caroline Florentia, elder daughter of the late William Watts of Hanslope Park. Her brother, Edward Hanslope Watts, is still remembered in North Buckinghamshire as the squire who was shot dead in 1912 by his own gamekeeper. Her sister Frederica and, in later years, her cousin Diana were to be regular visitors to the Bulls' house in Buckingham.

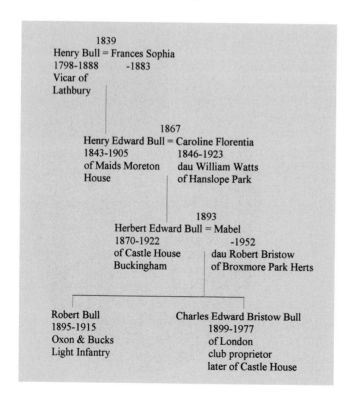

```
                    1839
         Henry Bull = Frances Sophia
         1798-1888        -1883
         Vicar of
         Lathbury
                    |
                    |
                              1867
              Henry Edward Bull = Caroline Florentia
              1843-1905           1846-1923
              of Maids Moreton    dau William Watts
              House               of Hanslope Park
                           |
                                   1893
                    Herbert Edward Bull = Mabel
                    1870-1922                -1952
                    of Castle House     dau Robert Bristow
                    Buckingham          of Broxmore Park Herts
              |_____|
              |                            |
      Robert Bull              Charles Edward Bristow Bull
      1895-1915                      1899-1977
      Oxon & Bucks                   of London
      Light Infantry                 club proprietor
                                     later of Castle House
```

40 Bull family tree.

Henry Edward and Caroline Florentia Bull rented Tickford Park, the big house south of the river at Newport Pagnell. Their son Herbert Edward was born there in 1870. A family photograph album, now in the Buckinghamshire Record Office, commences with two photographs of the house.[1] There are many photographs of Henry Edward taking part in cricket matches across the county, particularly at Shardeloes, the Amersham home of the Tyrwhitt Drake family. Henry Edward and his wife were well-known figures in the hunting field. He prided himself on his skill in handling coach horses and his opinion on a horse was always valued. He was a prominent figure at all county functions, and organised a series of county balls.

41   Henry Edward Bull, 1905.

By 1877 Henry Edward Bull and his wife Caroline Florentia had moved to The Cottage, a large house at the head of Castle Street, Buckingham, now numbered 12 and known as Hill House. This house had once belonged to Philip Box, the banker, and had been occupied by his nephew, Philip Box, and later by Philip's widow Penelope. About 1893, Henry Edward Bull moved to Maids Moreton House, a newly built house accessed by a long drive on the east side of Main Street, Maids Moreton. In 1901 Frederica Watts was living with the Bulls at Maids Moreton House. Henry Edward Bull died in 1905 and was buried at Lathbury. His widow Caroline Florentia continued to live at Maids Moreton until her death in 1923. Maids Moreton House was sold in 1924.

Herbert Edward Bull

Herbert Edward, son of Henry Edward and Caroline Florentia Bull, was educated at Eton. He married, in 1893, Mabel, daughter of the late Robert Bristow, of Broxmore Park, Whiteparish, Wiltshire. Their eldest son, Robert Edward Bristow

42   Herbert Edward Bull, 1907

Bull, was born in Brighton in 1895, and educated at Malvern and Sandhurst. He died at Festubert on 16 May 1915. There is a memorial to him in Maids Moreton church. Their younger son, Charles Edward Bristow Bull, was born at Buckingham in 1899. By this time Herbert Edward Bull had become a director of the Aylesbury Brewery Company and he and his young family were living at the Brewery House, 4 Castle Street, Buckingham. The Aylesbury firm had taken over the smaller Buckingham Brewery, situated between Castle Street and School Lane, in 1896.[2] Although the owner, Frank Higgins, was given a directorship in the Aylesbury Brewery Company, his manager, William Coran, was given notice and committed suicide.[3]

When Castle House came on the market in 1903, Herbert Edward Bull was able to purchase what was undoubtedly the most prestigious house in Buckingham. The purchase price of the house and 25 acres of land to the north was £4,700. The cost was partly offset by raising a loan of £3,500 from the vendor, Thomas Risley Hearn, and his brother-in-law, Edward Henry Thomas Fewson Small. This mortgage was not paid off until 1924.[4]

Like his father, Herbert Edward Bull was a keen sportsman, and founded or supported many local cricket, football and golf clubs. He was Secretary of the Buckinghamshire County Cricket Club and President of the Buckingham and District Football League. He was also one of the founders of the Buckingham Fire Brigade. He was a Conservative and served briefly as a member of Buckingham Town Council.

43   Castle House, 1912.

The Royal Commission on Historical Monuments

In 1912 Castle House was surveyed by the Royal Commission on Historical Monuments (RCHM). The investigator, J. Murray Kendall, made a thorough inspection, making notes on all the principal rooms and taking photographs of the exterior, the Great Parlour and the attics in the west wing. Unfortunately, Mr Kendall did not look at the east wing, which was at that time occupied by a tenant. Kendall thought the house was 'of considerable interest as it contained the remains of a medieval house of some importance'. His description is as follows:

The present House forms an irregular L but so late as 1835 it is reported that there were four ranges about a courtyard of which the present house formed the S. and W. range. The earliest detail now visible is of late 15th or early 16th century date and is contained in the W. wing which was part of the Hall range of the original house. The present S. wing is on the site, probably, of the Solar range; the kitchens and offices etc must have been in the destroyed N. range. The greater part if not the whole of the Hall remains in the W. wing but considerably altered. The Hall was apparently on the first floor for the present first floor appears to be of the 15th or 16th century.

The outside of the W. wing (the Hall) is thickly coated with modern plaster and is also partly covered by a lean-to addition on the E. The only [evidence] of the earlier detail visible is in the two windows in the W. wall of the Hall. These are each of two transomed cinquefoiled lights with tracery under square main heads and the heads, jambs and mullions are moulded outside and rebated for shutters inside. At the N. end of the wing is a modern bay window in which is inserted a stone inscribed WLM 1623 set within a circle. All other external detail is modern or 18th century. The street front of early 18th century date is a very handsome piece of work.

The Great Parlour (on ground floor in W. wing) is of three bays. At S. end is a large mantelpiece dated 1619. The fireplace has an 18th century grate. The overmantle rests on twisted oak Corinthian columns and is in two stages. The lower stage has bulging square baluster pilasters which divide it into three bays; between the pilasters are square and L shape carved panels; in the middle one is inscribed ANO 1619 WL ML. The top stage is in two bays with pairs of small Doric half-columns enriched with arabesques. The panels have pairs of round arches all richly carved. Above this is a very heavy enriched cornice and frieze. The ceiling has hollow chamfered wall plates and beams and the cross beams have angle bracketing with spandrel tracery and moulded corbels, all of c.1500 but much restored. In the W. wall are two windows (see elevations, At the N. end of the E. wall is a doorway of late 15th or early 16th century date, perhaps the E. doorway of the screens from the courtyard. It is now covered by a modern addition. The doorway has a pointed head and is continuously moulded with a double-ogee on the outside.

First Floor. A room at the N. end of the W. wing is lined with plain early 17th century panelling and has a frieze of long panels carved with arabesques. A room in the 18th century (S.) wing, at the W. end, is lined with reset early 17th century panelling.

Attic. The remains of three trusses of the open timber roof of the 15th or 16th century Hall are still visible. They are of queen post type with cambered and moulded tie and straining beams, purlins, etc. and angle bracketing; above the straining beams were carved members strutting the collar beams, with cupsed undersides; the trusses have been much cut up and defaced to allow passage through the attic. There are curved wind braces.[5]

44   The Great Parlour, 1912.

45   Roof timbers in the West
Wing, 1912.

Herbert Edward Bull, of Castle House, Buckingham, made his will on 7 May 1921. He left all his real and personal estate to trustees who were to sell the property and pay the income from the proceeds to his wife Mabel Bull until her death or remarriage. They were also to pay out of the income an annuity of £400 per year to his son Charles Edward Bristow Bull during his life. There was a proviso that the trustees might postpone the sale of the property at their own discretion.

Herbert Edward Bull died on 4 July 1922. The *Buckingham Advertiser*, on 8 July, in reporting his death, suggested that 'the death of the elder son, Mr Robert Bull, in 1915 while serving with the Oxford and Bucks Light Infantry in France, was a great shock to Mr Bull, who had never been of a really robust constitution. He was managing director and vice-chairman of the Aylesbury Brewery Company and a Justice of the Peace for Bucks.' He was buried at Lathbury. His will was proved 2 September 1922 by Mabel Bull and Charles Edward Bristow Bull. The effects were valued at only £7,548 3s. 11d.

Mabel Bull

In the event, Herbert Edward Bull's property was not sold and his widow, Mabel Bull, continued to live at Castle House. She had been a socialite in her youth, and lived in some style at Castle House, being particularly fond of hats and hat pins. In later life she took to her four-poster bed and her chain smoking produced a large nicotine stain on the ceiling. Mabel Bull's constant companion was the elegant and vivacious Diana Cunningham, who called Mabel Bull her 'granny' but whose real relationship to the Bull family was a good deal more complicated. In 1867 Henry Edward Bull had married Caroline Florentia, daughter of the late William Watts, of Hanslope Park. His mother-in-law, William's widow Caroline, married again, and had several children by her new husband, Reginald Walpole, who moved into Hanslope Park. One of these children, Caroline Emily Walpole, born at Hanslope Park in 1860, married a Scottish engineer named William Martin Cunningham, who spent many years working in Russia. His son, Martin Walpole Martin Cunningham, born in 1883, became a Russia merchant and married Zenia, who was said to have been a Russian countess. Their daughter, born in Russia in 1920, was named Diana Zenia Walpole Martin Cunningham. Probably because of the early death of her mother, Diana Cunningham came to live with Mabel Bull at Castle House about 1924.

Diana Cunningham was described by Mabel Bull's neighbour and friend, Dr John Bostock, as 'quite sensible but a bit wild'. He remarked on her wonderfully silky hair. Diana Cunningham married Norman Bragg in 1941 but, having divorced soon afterwards, married Edward Clement Wharton-Tigar in 1946. Wharton-Tigar was a director of Selection Trust, a mining conglomerate with interests all over the world. During the war he had worked for SOE (Special Operations Executive).[6] He and Diana were amongst the chief mourners at the 1952 funeral of Mabel Bull. Their wreath had the puzzling inscription 'Granny, in ever loving and most grateful memory, for so many kindnesses to us all'. The Wharton-Tigars lived in Kensington and had two daughters, Caroline, born in 1947, and Anne, born in 1948. E.C. Wharton-Tigar died in 1995, having left his world-famous collection of cigarette cards to the British Museum.

Charles Edward Bristow Bull

In Buckingham, Mabel Bull's son, Charles Edward Bristow Bull, was nicknamed 'Micky', but in London's clubland he was known as 'John' or 'Johnny'. In 1924 he was living at Cumberland Mansions, Hyde Park. 'John' Bull was flamboyant and sociable, and ran a succession of clubs frequented by actors and actresses. In December 1930 Charles Edward Bristow Bull, then of George Street, Portman Square, W., was fined £150 and costs for selling alcoholic liquor without a licence at Johnny's Club, Coventry Street, W.[7] In May 1932, Charles Edward Bristow Bull of 94 George Street, Portman Square, London W. and 4 & 5 Gerrard Street, Shaftesbury Avenue, London W.,

46 Diana Wharton-Tigar (née Cunningham), on 'Buckles', *c*.1940.

club manager, was declared bankrupt.[8] Charles Edward's financial affairs were not settled until 1934 when he and his mother raised a £500 mortgage on Castle House, which was later assigned to the Public Trustee. His debts were paid in full and he was released from bankruptcy in September 1934.[9] 'John' Bull continued his life as a club owner and socialite. In August 1938 Charles Edward Bristow Bull, then of Archer Street, London W1, was fined £10 and costs for supplying drinks at the Globe Club, Anchor Street during prohibited hours, and £10 for permitting gaming on the club premises.[10]

'John' Bull counted amongst his friends Laurence Olivier and Ivor Novello. He was particularly friendly with the actor, Pat Woodings, who was Ivor Novello's stage manager. Woodings' wife, Valerie, now aged 94, remembers John Bull well. The couple were regular

47 Castle House, 1948.

visitors to Castle House where John Bull entertained lavishly. He was a good cook, laid out an elegant dinner table and made regular visits to the wine cellar. He was well dressed but tended to wear sandals with no socks. Pat and Valerie Woodings holidayed with John Bull at Roquebrune, near Menton on the Italian border. He was godfather to their two daughters Rosemary and Penny.

During the Second World War, Castle House was home to about a dozen young women working at Bletchley Park, where German military signals were decoded. Several of the girls became close friends of the Bull family. Some of them returned after the war with their families to visit Mabel Bull and her son 'Micky'. One of these was Mary Pinkerton (née Grove), and 'Micky' Bull was godfather to her children.

48   'John' Bull in Scoutmaster's uniform, *c*.1950.

Council Houses

In 1944 Buckingham Borough made a compulsory purchase order under the 1936 Housing Act, buying 22½ acres of land belonging to Mabel Bull and Charles Edward Bristow Bull, immediately behind Castle House. The land was valued at £2,600. The council houses on Western Avenue and Overn Avenue were built on this land. The conveyance was dated 16 March 1946. Of the purchase money, £500 went to the Public Trustee, but the remaining £2,100 was no doubt a welcome injection of cash into the Bull household.[11]

On the 1946 conveyance, Charles Edward Bristow Bull gave his address as Castle House, Buckingham, where he lived with his mother for the next few years. He was friendly with the racing driver, Stirling Moss, who often stayed at Castle House when driving at Silverstone. 'Micky' Bull was also keen on amateur dramatics and put on several shows, including *Puss in Boots* and *Jack and*

49   'John' Bull, with Rosemary Woodings (now Carter), at Castle House, 1962.

50   On the stairs at Castle House, 1962. From left to right: Paddy Wilby, Penny Dover, Rosemary Woodings, 'John' Bristow Bull, Valerie Woodings, Geoffrey Dover.

the Bean Stalk, in a fives court in the buildings to the west of Castle House. On one occasion he is said to have built Cinderella's coach in his mother's kitchen and then found that it was too large to get through the door. The proceeds of these shows paid for the training of a guide dog for the blind each year.

Mabel Bull died on 5 January 1952. The *Buckingham Advertiser* recalled that she had come to live in Buckingham in 1893 on her marriage to Herbert Edward Bull, and that the couple had been leading lights in local and county society. She had been a particular supporter of the Buckingham Hospital. Mabel Bull was buried at Lathbury. Her son 'Micky' did not sell Castle House and it remained his home until 1963. In October of that year the local auctioneers, George Bennett & Co., held an auction of his furniture at Castle House. In January 1964 the house and 25 acres of land behind were sold to Buckingham Borough Council for £15,000. On the conveyance, Charles Edward Bristow Bull gave his address as formerly of Castle House, West Street, Buckingham, but then care of his solicitors, Beachcroft & Co., 29 Bedford Square, London. Castle House itself is only briefly described, but particular attention is paid to the rights connected with the private supply of water from the conduit house:

> All that piece or parcel of land situate adjoining West Street in the Borough and County of Buckingham together with the mansion house dwelling houses and buildings erected thereon or on some part or parts thereof and known as Castle House West Street Buckingham & numbers 9 and 10 West Street Buckingham on the plan annexed thereto and thereon coloured pink
>
> And also all that stone building known as the Conduit House shown and so marked on a plan annexed to a mortgage dated 28 May 1934 and made between[1] Mabel Bull and Charles Edward Bristow Bull[2] Mabel Bull[3] Charles Edward Bristow Bull[4] Keith Holcombe Johnson & John Heriot May and the conduit pipe leading from the same to Castle House aforesaid and all rights and easements connected therewith or with the said conduit pipe and in particular the right to repair the said pipe and for that purpose or for any other purpose relating to the said flow of water to take up and remove the soil of the said land through which the said pipe passes and to do all acts and to make and maintain the forcing plate connected to the said pipe of the flow of water through the same and to do and execute all acts and all works necessary for the purposes aforesaid or any of them all which said property (other than the said Conduit House and conduit pipe) was for the purpose of identification only edged pink on the plan annexed thereto.[12]

After the sale of Castle House 'Micky' Bull spent many years in France, but

51   'John' Bull in the garden of Castle House.

On Instructions from C. E. JOHN BRISTOW-BULL, Esq.

" CASTLE HOUSE "
BUCKINGHAM

Catalogue

of the

Antique   Furnishings

of the above Residence

which will be sold by Auction on the Premises

by Messrs.

BENNETT, SONS & BOND

on

WEDNESDAY, 9th OCTOBER, 1963

commencing at 10.30 a.m. precisely

ON VIEW MONDAY, 7th OCTOBER—11 a.m to 3 p.m.

Licensed Buffet (no break for Lunch)

ADMISSION to VIEW and SALE by CATALOGUE ONLY (2/6 each) which may be obtained upon application to the Auctioneers, Messrs. Bennett, Sons & Bond, Auction Offices, Market Hill, Buckingham. (Tel. 2104).

52   Sale of furniture, Castle House, October 1963.

53   Castle House, 1978.

54   Castle House, East Wing, *c*.1978.

55 Castle House, West Wing, c.1978.

56 Panelling in the 'King's Chamber', c.1978.

57 Castle House, bay window, West Wing, c.1978.

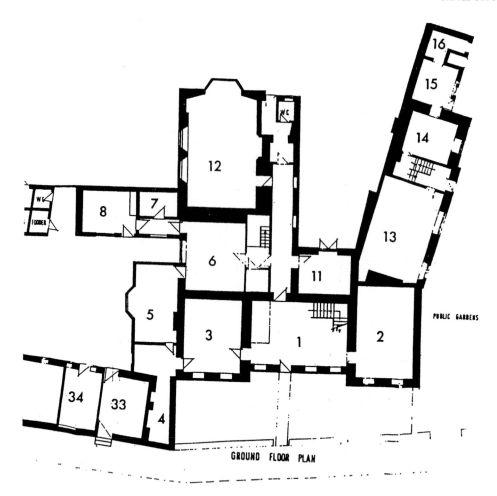

GROUND FLOOR PLAN

WEST STREET A 422

GROUND FLOOR: **3,183 sq. ft.**

1.	Entrance Hall (S)	15'10 x 24'
2.	Rent Office (S)	23'6 x 14'10
3.	Mayour's Parlour (S)	14'10 x 18'7
4.	Pantry	11'6 x 16'9
5.	Office (W)	20' x 11'
6.	Old Kitchen/Store	15'2 x 16'9
7.	Store	6' x 9'6
8.	Boiler Room	10' x 13'
9.	Passage Way	—
10.	Cloakroom & WC	—
11.	Office (N)	13' x 10'
12.	Council Chamber (N & W)	17'10 x 32' overall
13.	St. John Ambulance Room (E)	24'9 x 13'1
14.	Office (E)	10'7 x 12'
15.	Kitchen (E)	11' x 8'6
16.	Pantry	9'6 x 6'8

58   Ground-floor plan, Castle House, 1978.

FIRST FLOOR: **2,043 sq. ft.**

No.	Room	Dimensions
17.	Print Room (E)	10'1 x 8'4
18.	Office (E)	11'3 x 12'3
19.	Office (E)	12'3 x 9'7
20.	Passage Way	—
21.	Cloakroom & WC	—
22.	Office (S)	15'5 x 14'11
23.	Landing	—
24.	Office (S)	16' x 13'3
25.	Office (S)	14'10 x 15'5
26.	Passage Way & Stores	—
27.	Cloakroom & WC	—
28.	Office (W)	10' x 14'4
29.	Office (W)	15'10 x 8'4
30.	Office (W)	20'6 x 14'5
31.	Office (N & W)	21'2 x 18' overall
32.	Office (N)	17'10 x 6'9

59   First-floor plan, Castle House, 1978.

60   The Council Chamber, 1978.

61   Carved fireplace, Council
Chamber, 1978.

62 The Mayor's Parlour, 1978.

towards the end of his life he returned to London. His last address was 4 Joanna House, Worlidge Street, London W6. He died in hospital on 16 October 1977.

Buckingham Borough Council

Buckingham Borough Council used Castle House as offices from 1963 until Buckingham became a part of Aylesbury Vale District at local government reorganisation in 1974. The room on the left of the main hallway became the Mayor's Parlour, whilst the room on the right became the Rent Office. The large room on the ground floor of the West Wing became the Council Chamber. The East Wing, which the Bulls had leased to the solicitor Martin Athay, was converted into offices, the largest of which was occupied by the St John Ambulance Brigade. In 1971 the Borough Council opened the garden on the east of the house to the public. It became a popular place of resort, especially at lunchtimes.

In April 1974, following the Conservative government's local government reorganisation, Buckingham Borough was absorbed by the newly created Aylesbury Vale District Council. The new body showed little sensitivity to local civic pride and decided to demolish Buckingham Town Hall and to sell Castle House. The Town Hall was saved after vigorous local protests, but the sale of Castle House went ahead in 1978. The sale particulars described Castle House as a fine period property providing 5,250 sq. ft. of prestige offices set in grounds of 1.48 acres, suitable fore residential, institutional, educational, nursing home or hostel accommodation. The house was sold with planning permission for the conversion of the courtyard and outbuildings into two flats and three houses. The purchaser was Barbara Mary Edmondson, then of 23 Cunningham Hill Road, St Albans, wife of Derek Edmondson. The property was conveyed by Aylesbury Vale District Council to Mrs Edmondson on 8 December 1978. She paid the asking price of £65,000.

Oddly for such a prestigious property, the deed parcel passed to Barbara Edmondson in 1978 contains no documents earlier than the 1934 mortgage of Castle House by Mabel and Charles Edward Bristow Bull. Aylesbury Vale District Council's deed parcel to the land behind Castle House contains nothing earlier than the 1904 conveyance from Thomas Risley Hearn to Herbert Edward Bull. If any reader of this book should ever come across any earlier deeds, particularly the mysterious 1837 conveyance to the solicitor, Thomas Hearn, Mrs Edmondson will be delighted to hear of it.

BIBLIOGRAPHY

Barton, M.H., *A Barton Family*, 1982

Beckett, J., *The Rise and Fall of the Grenvilles*, 1994

Bonner, D.C. and Vernon, M.T., *Buckingham*, 1970

Clarke, John, *The Book of Buckingham*, 1984

Davis, R.W., *Political change and continuity, Buckinghamshire 1760-1885*, 1972

Elliott, Douglas J., *Buckingham: the Loyal and Ancient Borough*, 1975

Gibbs, Robert, *Buckinghamshire Local Occurences*, 1882

Gibbs, Robert, *Worthies of Buckinghamshire*, 1888

Harrison, J.T., *Leisure Hour Notes on Historical Buckingham*, 1909

Hunt, Julian, *Pictorial History of Buckingham*, 1994

Lipscomb, George, *History and Antiquities of the County of Buckingham*, 4 vols, 1847

Page, William (ed.), *Victoria History of the County of Buckingham*, 4 vols, 1905-27

Pevsner, Nikolaus, *Buildings of England: Buckinghamshire*, 2nd ed., 1994

Pike, W.T. (ed.), *Berks, Bucks and Beds in the 20th century*, contemporary biographies, 1907

Poornan, Paul K., *The Royal Latin School*, Buckingham, 2001

Press, C.A. Manning, *Buckinghamshire Leaders, Social and Political*, 1905

Reed, Michael, *Buckinghamshire Landscape*, 1979

Reed, Michael, *History of Buckinghamshire*, 1993

Roundell, H., *Some Account of the Town of Buckingham*, 1857

Roundell, H., *Buckingham Town, Buckingham People and their Neighbours during the Civil Wars*, 1864

Royal Commission on the Historical Monuments *Inventory of the Historical Monuments in Buckinghamshire*, 2 vols 1912-13

Sheahan, James, *History and Topography of Buckinghamshire*, 1862

Silvester, Henry, *History of Buckingham*, c.1845 (mss Bucks Archaeological Society)

Verney, M. (ed.), *Verney letters of the 18th century*, 1930

Willis, Browne, *History and Antiquities of the Town, Hundred and Deanery of Buckingham*, 1755

NOTES

Introduction – What's in a Name?

1. Thomas Silvester, *History of Buckingham*, 1829, mss Buckinghamshire Archaeological Society.
2. E.M. Elvey, 'The History of Nos 1 and 2, Market Hill, Buckingham', *Records of Bucks*, Vol. XX, Part 3, 1977, p.305.
3. Centre for Buckinghamshire Studies, DX/2/21.
4. C.B.S., D1/9/8.

Chapter 1 – Location, Location, Location

1. Will of Simon Lambert of Buckingham P.C.C. 1618.
2. Will of Sir Edward Richardson of Buckingham P.C.C. 1637.
3. Sale Catalogue, 1903 C.B.S.
4. J.G. Jenkins (ed.), Calendar of the Roll of the Justices on Eyre, 1227, *Buckinghamshire Record Society*, Vol. 6, 1945, p.62.
5. Page, W. (ed.), *Victoria History of the County of Buckingham*, vol. i, p.392, vol. iii, p.486.

Chapter 2 – Farmers and Lawyers

1. Douglas J. Elliot, *Buckingham: the Loyal and Ancient Borough*, London and Chichester, Phillimore & Co. Ltd, 1975, p.16.
2. F. Markham, *History of Milton Keynes and District*, 1973, vol. i, p.114.
3. J.G. Jenkins, 'An Early Coroners Role for Buckinghamshire', *Records of Bucks*, 13, 1934-40, pp.163-85.
4. G. Lipscombe, *History and Antiquities of the County of Buckingham*, 1847, vol. iii, p.14.
5. G. Lipscomb, *op. cit.*, vol.i, pp.xxi-xxii.
6. A. Goodman, 'Richard II's servants and the Missenden Inheritance', *Records of Bucks*, Vol. 17, 1961-5, pp.350-5.
7. *VCH Buckinghamshire*, vol. ii, p.145.
8. L. Boatwright, 'Inquests and Indictments from late 14th century Buckinghamshire' *Buckinghamshire Record Society*, 29, 1994, p.xxxix
9. Roskell, *op. cit.*, pp.138-43.
10. *VCH Buckinghamshire*, vol. iii, p.485.
11. G. Lipscomb, *op. cit.* vol.i, pp.xxi-xxii.
12. Browne Willis, *The History and Antiquities of the Town, Hundred and Deanery of Buckingham*, London, 1755, p.54.
13. *Cokes Reports*, 1738, Part IV, p.96.
14. Browne Willis, *op. cit.*, p.301.

15. G.R. Elvey, 'Luffield Priory Charters', *Buckinghamshire and Northamptonshire Record Societies*, 2 volumes, 1975, volume ii, p.328.
16. A.F. Leach, *The Schools of Medieval England*, London, Methuen, 1969, p.253.
17. Eleanora Dayrell, *The History of the Dayrells of Lillingtone Dayrell*, Jersey, 1885, p.4.
18. J.I. Catto and R. Evans (eds), *The History of the University of Oxford*, Oxford, Clarendon Press, 1992.
19. K.A. Vickers, *England in the late Middle Ages*, London, Methuen & Co., 1913, pp.495-6.
20. Colin Platt, *Medieval England: A Social History and Archaeology from the Conquest to 1600 AD*, London, Book Club Associates, 1978, p.138.
21. British Library Additional Charters 217.

Chapter 3 – Queens and Courts

1. Garrett Mattingly, *Catherine of Aragon*, London, Jonathan Cape, 1942, p.121.
2. A.C. Chibnall (ed.), 'The Certificate of Musters', *Records of Buckinghamshire*, Vol. 17, 1973.
3. *VCH Bedfordshire*, vol. iii, pp.433-4.
4. *VCH Bedfordshire*, vol. iii, p.406.
5. Josiah C. Wedgwood, *History of Parliament: Biographies of Members of the House of Commons 1439-1509*, London, HMSO, 1936, p.352.
6. George Lipscombe, *History and Antiquities of the County of Bucks*, 1847, p.569.
7. H.W. Chapman, *The Last Tudor King*, London, Jonathan Cape, 1961, pp.197-217.
8. S.T. Bindoff, *The History of Parliament; The House of Commons 1509-1558*, London, Secker and Warburg, 1982, Volume II, pp.166-7.
9. C.B.S. D/C/4/100.
10. The English Reports, volume LXXVI, Kings Bench Division V, Containing Coke, Parts 1, 2, 3, and 4, William Green & Sons, Edinburgh, Stevens & Sons, London, 1907, pp.1079-80.
11. Douglas J. Elliott, *Buckingham: the Loyal and Ancient Borough*, Chichester, Phillimore, 1973, pp. 240-1.
12. Coke's Reports.
13. *Ibid.*, p.1080.
14. *Ibid.*, pp.1080-5.
15. *Ibid.*, p.1085.
16. *Ibid.*, p.1086.

17. *Ibid.*, p.1087.
18. *Ibid.*, p.1090.
19. *Ibid.*, pp.1091-92.
20. *Ibid.*, p.1091.
21. *Ibid.*, p.1092.
22. *Ibid.*, p.1094.
23. *Ibid.*, p.1095.

Chapter 4 – Stuart Splendour: Court and City

1. Sir Francis Crawley (1584-1649) of Luton, Bedfordshire. Studied at Gray's Inn. Serjeant at Law, 1623. One of the Counsel for the Earl of Bristol, 1626. Justice of Common Pleas, 1632. Supported the legality of Ship Money and gave judgement for the King against Hampden. Impeached by Parliament, 1641. With the King at Oxford during the Civil War.
2. P.R.O. Ministers Accounts, bundle 759, No. 27.
3. William Camden (ed. Gibson), *Britannia* Vol. I, p.311.
4. Hundred Rolls (Records Commission), Vol. I, p.29.
5. C.B.S., B.A.S. Deeds 6/35.
6. C.B.S., B.A.S. Deeds 6/174.
7. C.B.S., B.A.S. Deeds 6/34.
8. James T. Harrison, *Leisure Hour Notes on Historical Buckingham*, 1909, p.57.
9. P.R.O., C142/429/118.
10. P.R.O., C142/429/125.
11. Rev. H. Roundell, *Some Account of the Town of Buckingham* (1857), pp.12-13.
12. *Ibid.*
13. Douglas Elliot, *Buckingham: the Loyal and Ancient Borough*, pp.113-14.
14. Rev. Henry Roundell, *Buckingham Town, Buckingham People and their Neighbours during the Civil Wars*, Aylesbury, A Pickbum, 1864, pp.30-1.
15. For Clarendon's account of Charles' time in Buckingham see W. Dunn Macray (ed.), Edward, Earl of Clarendon, *The History of the Rebellion and Civil Wars in England*, Oxford, Oxford University Press, 1888, volume III, pp.363-5.
16. Stamford lies far from the line of the direct route from Buckingham to Blithfield, which follows Watling Street from Towcester to Tamworth. The reason why Harvey Bagot was taken to Stamford was that his father's step-mother's family, the Caves, lived there.
17. On 21 October 1687. He was buried in the Church of All Hallows on the Wall, London.

Chapter 5 – The Rogers Family: Brewing and Rebuilding.

1. *Victoria History of the County of Buckingham*, vol. iii, 1925, p.469.
2. *VCH Bucks*, vol. iv, 1927, p.419.
3. C.B.S., D/X/138.
4. Verney Papers, 2/1151.
5. Bucks Sessions Records, vol. ii, 1694-1705, p.436.
6. Centre for Kentish Studies, V 908/T 271/2.
7. Margaret Lady Verney (ed.), *Verney Letters of the 18th Century*, vol. 1, p.306.

8. London Metropolitan Archives, Misc. Deeds HMD/X/121.
9. Browne Willis, *History and Antiquities of the Town, Hundred and Deanery of Buckingham*, 1755, pp.34-6.
10. C.B.S., D225/13.
11. Sun Fire Insurance 8/12529.
12. Nikolaus Pevsner and Elizabeth Williamson, *The Buildings of England: Buckinghamshire*, 2nd ed., 1994, p.202.
13. C.B.S., D225/34.
14. John Carswell, *The South Sea Bubble*, 1961, p.278.
15. Sun Fire Insurance 6/8317.
16. Sun Fire Insurance 8/5254,5256.
17. Sun Fire Insurance 8/12509.
18. Sun Fire Insurance 7/10526-8.
19. Sun Fire Insurance 19/35093.
20. Thomas Silvester Mss., *History of Buckingham*, 1829, mss Buckinghamshire Archaeological Society, vol.ii, p.3.
21. Sun Fire Insurance 19/35095.
22. Sun Fire Insurance 19/35094.
23. Sun Fire Insurance 28/48472.
24. Browne Willis, *op. cit.*, p.53.
25. Verney Papers, 2/1157-9.
26. *Verney Letters of the 18th Century*, vol. 2, p.191.
27. Sun Fire Insurance 116/154580.
28. Royal Insurance 5/775539.

Chapter 6 – The Theeds and Shillingfords: Gentlemen Farmers

1. C.B.S., D/X/2/21.
2. *Ibid.*
3. Sun Insurance 329/504469.
4. C.T. Martin, *Catalogue of the Archives of All Souls College*, 1877.
5. Verney Papers 2/1100.
6. C.T. Martin, *op. cit.*
7. C.B.S., Padbury Enclosure Award.
8. C.B.S., D/X/2/21.
9. C.B.S., D/1/9/8.
10. C.B.S., D/X/2/21.

Chapter 7 – The Boxes: Banking and the Irish Mystery

1. C.B.S., D 225/34.
2. Verney Papers 2/1099.
3. C.B.S., Plans of Farms in Bourton Manor belonging to Earl Verney n.d. DX/403.
4. Verney Papers 2/1099.
5. C.B.S., B/Buc/5/1/2.
6. Royal Exchange Insurance 7/83984.
7. G.E.C., *Complete peerage*, vol. 5, p. 296
8. Anne Fremantle (ed.), *The Wynne Diaries*, 1940, vol. iii, pp.94-5.
9. James Harrison, *Leisure Hour Notes on Historical Buckingham*, 1909, p.97.
10. C.B.S., D/X/1/50.
11. Sack, James J., *The Grenvillites*, Illinois University Press, 1979, p.31; Huntington Library, HEH STG Box 123 Box to Buckingham 14 Aug 1813.

Chapter 8 – The Hearns: The Law and the Profits

1. Sun Fire Insurance 324/497186.
2. Verney Papers 2/1099.
3. Richard W. Davies, *Political Change and Continuity 1760-1885, a Buckinghamshire Study*, 1972, p.130.
4. C.B.S., S/136/11.
5. C.B.S., D/136/3.
6. C.B.S., D/FR/136/18.
7. *Illustrated London News*, 25 January 1845, p.52.
8. Aylesbury Vale District Council deeds to Western Avenue.
9. Rev. Thomas Silvester, *Manuscript History of Buckingham*, 1829, mss Buckinghamshire Archaeological Society, vol. ii, p.93.
10. *Records of Buckinghamshire*, Vol. v, 1884, p.415-16.
11. C.B.S., D/WIG/2/6/450.

Chapter 9 – The Bulls: Beer and Champagne

1. C.B.S., D/114 Add.
2. Kelly's *Directory of Aylesbury*, 1913.
3. *Buckingham Advertiser*, 8 October 1896.
4. File on Castle House, RCHM Swindon.
5. Aylesbury Vale District Council deeds to Western Avenue.
6. Edward Wharton-Tigar, *Burning Bright*, 1987.
7. *The Times*, 19 December 1930.
8. AVDC deeds.
9. *London Gazette*, 25 September 1934.
10. *The Times*, 13 August 1938.
11. AVDC deeds.
12. *Ibid*.

INDEX